Studio Review Jan 2012
George Simpson Visiting
Critic Mike Cadwell
Image: Rachel Travers

PARA-Situation [X]

THE [LOVING] METROPOLITAN LANDSCAPE

Architecture, Landscape and The Ecosophic Object

DORIAN WISZNIEWSKI

Introduction: Place and Work

The work in this book comes from two Post Graduate design-led research studios at the Edinburgh School of Architecture and Landscape Architecture (ESALA): the first year of the two-year Master of Architecture and the one-year M Sc Architectural and Urban Design Programmes. The projects promote the interaction between architectural, urban and landscape sensibilities.

This book acts as the first of two volumes. This volume is seen as an introduction to some of the research themes and the specific issues of the situations under investigation. The work has been developed through the interaction between a large number of researchers: 19 students and 8 staff from the Alghero School of Architecture, Sardinia, and 47 students (26 M Arch and 21 M Sc) and 4 staff from the University of Edinburgh. It has also benefitted from participation by various international scholars. The second volume, to be produced in due course, will develop from this point and present projects that focus on particular research themes in yet richer detail.

There are three main themes under investigation. Two of them are elaborated a little through short texts in this volume: Architecture, Landscape and The Ecosophic Object and The [Loving] Metropolitan Landscape. The attitude towards the third theme — PARA-Situation — is articulated and framed through the presentation of the book. The themes take their impetus from a range of political philosophers who make especially rich efforts to invigorate and overlap phenomenological and critical impulses. The book and work celebrate difference whilst being clearly placed in specific cultural situations and discourses. As Michel Serres puts it: "The prefix para is counted, calculated, weighed in its difference from equilibrium. But it is also placed and situated …"[1]

[DW]

1   Michel Serres, *The Parasite*, trans. Lawrence R. Schehr, 2007, pp.32–33.

Contents

1	Introduction: Place and Work	DW	4
2	Contents		5
3	Architecture, Landscape and The Ecosophic Object Mission Statement	DW	6
4	Architecture, Landscape and The Ecosophic Object	DW	10
	Architettura, Paesaggio e L'oggetto Ecosofico		13
5	The [Loving] Metropolitan Landscape (English)	DW	16
	The [Loving] Metropolitan Landscape (Italian)		18
6	PARA-Situation [X, Scotland]		22
7	Scenarios for Olbia / Scenari per Olbia	FR MV	lvi
9	PARA-Situation [X, OLBIA, Sardinia]		liv
10	Architectural Initiation	YH	clxiii
11	Bibliography		170
12	Credits		174

Mission Statement

THE (LOVING) METROPOLITAN LANDSCAPE

Architecture, Landscape and The Ecosophic Object'

1. Mission:

To resist the normalisation and making generic of otherwise specific practices and specific existential territories.

2. Means:

An understanding of the interrelation between The Three Ecologies:

The Environment

Social Relations

Human Subjectivity

3. The Interest:

To give opportunity to the "**ecosophic object**". The "incorporeal species" are in crisis. (p.82; n.2)

4. The concern:

(i) Integrated World Capitalism's (IWC) purpose seems to be about making more time — but Guattari asks "for what?" (p.82; n.3) We must take all necessary time to produce; we must resist reducing time of production so that we have time to do nothing.

(ii) Global Markets destroy "specific value systems." (p.20)

(ii) All social relations controlled by military/ industrial processes (a double pincer movement).

(iii) A "vague" sense of social belonging. Rather than acknowledge it, such vagueness pretends to be explicit and clear and denies or, at worst, fears its asperity (its texture and incompleteness; there is only ever an approximate sense of self, community and belonging). (p.21)

(iv) Alterity tends to lose its asperity (its texture, roughness): tourism, for example, usually amounts to no more than a journey on the spot (i.e. histories are recreated as "shows": simulacra)!

5. One of the Three Ecologies – Human Subjectivity:

Guattari has a "transversalist conception of subjectivity"; i.e. subjectivity ought to be encouraged to be transversalist:

Rather than an exclusive compartmentation of specialist conceptions of existence, be they ordinary or extraordinary existence, Guattari promotes a subjectivity that forms in the first instance from an active crossing between different life productions. Subjective compartmentation — the enemy - has an economic dimension, expressed clearly in the efficiency models of Fordist production through division of

[AH]

[AH]

[SH]

[AH]

[AH]

[BZ]

[SH]

[AH]

[BZ]

[AH]

VIETATO PASSARE O SOSTARE NEL RAGGIO D'AZIONE DELL'ESCAVATORE

MACCHINE IN MOVIMENTO

[AH]

[AH]

[AH]

THE [LOVING] METROPOLITAN LANDSCAPE

Architecture, Landscape and The Ecosophic Object

This is a research project that has involved academic relations between the School of Architecture at The University of Edinburgh (ESALA) and the Faculty of Architecture, Alghero/Sassari (Sardinia), Italy. It uses the notion of Metropolitan Landscape as an alternative to globalisation. The term globalisation is considered too loaded, too loose and too general to be practically useful for the contexts of this study. This is an architectural-urban study into The Metropolitan Landscape and Ecosophy. Reflection on the metropolitan landscape focuses the enquiry into the disposition of the urban and rural landscapes. The metropolitan landscape refers to relations between city and country, individual and community, as they operate as part of inter-region and inter-state politico-economic apparatus.

Marx quipped that capitalist urbanisation inverted the conventional relationship between the urban and rural landscape: paraphrasing, where once the rural population worked the land as the basis for making meals for both themselves and the urban population, under the asymmetrically weighted, bureaucratic and techno-instrumental forces of capital management and industrial production, the newly tuned capitalist urban imperative made a meal of the rustics.[1] As much as the city was developed to produce more, so was the countryside. As much as the factory workers were enslaved to division of labour, so were the rustics. Production from factories, fields and oceans was driven beyond the local markets of subsistence, desire and pleasure towards national and international commodification.

However, rather than see the ongoing relation between urban and rural landscapes as simplistically and dialectically opposed with concomitant master-plans,

---
1   Marx, Grundrisse, 1856. p 262

administered uncritically and slavishly, this study suggests that the relation can still be mutually complex, but it must also be caring. This study is directed towards The [*Loving*] Metropolitan Landscape. The metropolitan landscape is explored under specific themes and relations of care. Movement between Architecture, Landscape and Ecology holds the themes together. The principle theoretical impetus comes from a [paradoxical] search for the "ecosophic object." The ecosophic object is the tactical focus of how ecology is approached through this study, but also then of the relations between Architecture and Landscape. The ecosophic object, the product of ecological wisdom, requires that we approach ecology from a deep poetic and philosophical understanding of the interrelation between the environment, social practices and human subjectivity.[2]

Therefore, the study looks into different territorial models that care as much for how the city is an effect of landscape as the landscape is an effect of the urban. It tackles head-on the various crises and threats brought to bear on local value systems by historical and contemporary Global/European markets. The study looks into local, city, regional, state, national and international scales of operation. However, the purpose of the design-led research (in both institutions) is to find positive means by which the "incorporeal species" of creative production (the science of artistic, poetic, literary and other creative enterprises) help re-evaluate existing whilst developing the potential of new "existential territories" (e.g. houses, shops, social clubs, hospitals, museums, galleries, parks, food and waste infrastructures, energy networks and other constructions of social practice yet to be imagined).

Some findings of this research might be applied to different contexts and scales of metropolitan landscape. However, the study develops initially from two specific island contexts: the North and Western Islands of Scotland (Orkney and the Hebrides) and the island of Sardinia in the Mediterranean. These islands have very different ecologies, histories and magnitudes, but they illustrate similar tensions and provide similar potentially rich discourses within which design-led research propositions might be developed, for example: they are archipelagos with different magnitudes of islands and populations with clearly evident cultural, civic

Felix Guattari, *The Three Ecologies*, 2000.

and landscape relational histories; they each have ancient (Neolithic) archaeological sites, of international importance that continue to inspire contemporary consciousness; they have similar distribution of population densities (smaller urbanities proportional to greater landscapes and seascapes); as low density and smaller urbanities their local political power structures frequently operate in abstract relations to larger administrative metropolitan centres; both island contexts are affected by European Community "regional status" whilst having strong historical and contemporary claims for cultural and political independence from their nation states; the landscapes are historically multi-cultural and multi-lingual, with still pertinent contemporary issues that contest the privileging/marginalising of specific cultural identities; much of the landscape has been and is owned and developed by people who do not live there; they evidence similar tensions and opportunities between historical/ traditional land and sea economies and potential new leisure/tourist economies; they each have temporal/seasonal population fluctuations; they each have historical and contemporary strategic international locations, especially military; they each have specific geological and mineral resources of historical and contemporary significance; they each have proximity to deep-sea oil/gas resources; and they are both sites of pioneering research on renewable energies — wind, wave and solar power.

(DW)

THE [LOVING] METROPOLITAN LANDSCAPE

Architettura, Paesaggio e L'oggetto Ecosofico

Questo è un progetto di ricerca che coinvolge relazioni accademiche fra la Scuola di Architettura dell'Università di Edimburgo (ESALA) e la Facoltà di Architettura di Alghero dell'Università degli Studi di Sassari (Sardegna, Italia). Nel progetto si ricorre alla locuzione di Metropolitan Landscape per definire un concetto alternativo a quello della globalizzazione. Il termine globalizzazione, infatti, è ritenuto troppo carico, troppo ampio e troppo generale per essere effettivamente utilizzato nei contesti studiati. L'intero progetto è uno studio architettonico-urbanistico sul Metropolitan Landscape e sull' Ecosofia. La riflessione sul paesaggio metropolitano indaga il carattere dei paesaggi urbani e rurali e si riferisce ai rapporti fra città e campagna, fra individuo e comunità, come parte di un apparato inter-regionale, politico-economico e inter-statale.

Marx ironizza sull'inversione del tradizionale rapporto tra paesaggio urbano e rurale provocato dall'urbanizzazione capitalistica. Parafrasando, se un tempo la popolazione rurale lavorava la terra per produrre cibo per sé e per la popolazione urbana, ora, sotto le forze asimmetriche, burocratiche e tecnico-strumentali della gestione del capitale e della produzione industriale, il nuovo imperativo del capitalismo urbano si è cibato dei contadini. 1 Tanto quanto la città è stata sviluppata per produrre di più, altrettanto lo è stata la campagna. Tanto quanto gli operai sono stati ridotti in schiavitù, a causa della divisione del lavoro, altrettanto lo sono stati i contadini. La produzione ottenuta dalle fabbriche, dai campi e dagli oceani è stata spinta oltre i mercati locali della sussistenza, del desiderio e del piacere, verso la mercificazione nazionale e internazionale.

Tuttavia, invece di vedere la relazione in corso tra paesaggi urbani e rurali come semplicisticamente e dialetticamente opposti ai concomitanti masterplan – acriticamente e pedissequamente applicati – questo studio suggerisce che la relazione può essere ancora reciprocamente attenta e complessa. Questo studio è orientato al [Loving] Metropolitan Landscape. Il paesaggio metropolitano è esplorato attraverso temi specifici e relazioni di cura. La dinamica del lavoro dello studio, e quindi anche la dinamica della sua lettura, si muove fra Architettura, Paesaggio ed Ecologia, tiene loro insieme. La principale spinta teorica viene

1   Marx, *Grundrisse*, 1856.

PARA-Situation [X]
THE [LOVING] METROPOLITAN LANDSCAPE
Architettura, Paesaggio e L'oggetto Ecosofico

da una ricerca [paradossale] verso l'"oggetto ecosofico". L'oggetto ecosofico diventa il fulcro tattico per indagare l'ecologia,e,al contempo, i rapporti tra Architettura e Paesaggio. L'oggetto ecosofico, prodotto di una saggezza ecologica, richiede un approccio all'ecologia dotato di una profonda comprensione poetica e filosofica dell'interrelazione tra ambiente, pratiche sociali e soggettività umana.2

Pertanto, lo studio esamina diversi modelli territoriali che s'interessano della città come conseguenza del paesaggio e del paesaggio come conseguenza dell'urbano. Esso affronta a testa alta le varie crisi e le minacce esercitate sui sistemi di valori locali da parte dei mercati Globali / Europei, storici e contemporanei. Lo studio indaga le scale di funzionamento locale, cittadine, regionali, statali, nazionali e internazionali. Tuttavia, sia per la Scuola di Architettura di Edimburgo (ESALA) sia il Dipartimento di Architettura di Alghero, scopo della ricerca, per mezzo del progetto, è quello di individuare mezzi positivi con cui le "specie incorporee"3 della produzione creativa (la scienza delle azioni artistiche, poetiche, letterarie e altre attività creative) possano aiutare a rivalutare l'esistente e nel contempo a sviluppare il potenziale dei nuovi "territori esistenziali"4 (case, negozi, centri sociali, ospedali, musei, gallerie, parchi, infrastrutture del cibo e dei rifiuti, reti energetiche e altre costruzioni della pratica sociale).

Alcuni risultati di questa ricerca potrebbero essere applicati a diversi contesti e a diverse scale di paesaggio metropolitano anche se lo studio inizialmente ha interessato

2   Felix Guattari, *Le tre ecologie*, 1991.
3   Ibid.p..89.
4   Ibid.

due specifici ambiti insulari: le isole Settentrionali e Occidentali della Scozia (Orcadi e le Ebridi) e la Sardegna nel Mediterraneo. Queste isole hanno ecologie, storie e discorsi simili, ma manifestano tensioni e grandezze molto diverse, potenzialmente ricchi, entro i quali le proposizioni della ricerca basata sul progetto potrebbero essere sviluppate. Alcuni elementi in comune: sono entrambi arcipelaghi con isole di grandezze diverse e popolazioni con relazioni storiche culturali, civiche e di paesaggio ben evidente; ciascuna di esse ha antichi siti archeologici (del periodo Neolitico) d'importanza internazionale, che continuano ad alimentare la consapevolezza contemporanea; hanno una simile densità di popolazione (centri di modeste dimensioni in ampi paesaggi terrestri e marini); entrambi hanno centri a bassa le cui strutture del potere politico locale spesso operano attraverso relazioni astratte con i grandi centri amministrativi metropolitani; entrambi i contesti insulari, pur rivendicando, anche storicamente, l'indipendenza culturale e politica dai loro stati nazionali, sono interessati dallo "Status Regionale"5 della Comunità Europea; i paesaggi sono storicamente multi-culturali e multi-linguistici, con problemi contemporanei tuttora attinenti, che contestano l'atto di privilegiare /marginalizzare specifiche identità culturali; la trasformazione di gran parte di questi paesaggi è dovuta a coloro i quali, provenienti da altri luoghi, ne detengono la proprietà; essi mostrano tensioni e opportunità simili tra le economie storiche/ tradizionali della terra e del mare e le nuove economie potenziali per il leisure /turismo; entrambi hanno fluttuazioni temporali/stagionali della popolazione; entrambi possiedono siti, storici e contemporanei, di rilevanza strategica, in particolare dal punta di vista militare; entrambi hanno specifiche risorse geologiche e minerarie di importanza storica e contemporanea; entrambi hanno in prossimità dei loro mari risorse di petrolio/gas; infine entrambi sono siti di ricerca e sperimentazione pionieristica sulle energie rinnovabili (eolica, marina e solare).

(DW)

5   La Scozia e la Sardegna sono entrambe classificate come Regioni dalla EUR-Lex, organo legislativo dell'Unione Europea.

THE [LOVING] METROPOLITAN LANDSCAPE

The governance and organisation of our landscape is caught in a bind between overly simplistic paradigms of either high- or low-density urbanities: the models establish a dialectical relation between either larger urbanities containing pockets (archipelagos) of landscape and smaller urbanities surrounded by landscape, frequently using the latter to model the edges of the former. In most urban paradigms mass and density become the key features for organising urban ecology.[1] I challenge these reductive tendencies by shifting the territorial paradigm away from one of centre and edges to the notion of edges as being the re-current condition in a continuous and open landscape of different pre-occupations.

I use the term Metropolitan Landscape to give a sense of the urban to questions of landscape and that of landscape to questions of urbanity. The [Loving] Metropolitan Landscape does not differentiate the architectural impulse, the impulse to construct, which brings geometry (precise and inexact rulings) to all conditions of landscape, be they agrarian or urban. Echoing Giorgio Agamben, I suggest using the term metropolitan, "to designate the new urban [and agrarian] fabric that emerges in parallel with the processes of transformation that Michel Foucault defined as the shift from the territorial power of the ancient regime, of sovereignty, to modern biopower, that is in its essence governmental."[2] In Agamben's model, the relations between landscape and urbanism is conditioned by three types of dispositifs (apparatuses): First, reality as humans and

1   For example, see Aldo Rossi, Primary Elements and The Concept of Area, in The Architecture of The City (Cambridge MA: MIT Press, 1984) p.65.
2   Giorgio Agamben, Metropolis, translated from Audio files by Arianna Bove The European Graduate School, March 17 2007, http://www.egs.edu/faculty/giorgio-agamben/articles/metropolis/. My insertion [ ].

living beings as a developing series of dispositions between one and others; Second, "the dispositifs [apparatuses] that continuously capture and take hold of them"[3]; and "the third fundamental element that defines a dispositif... is the series of processes of subjectivation that result from the relation, the *corpo a corpo*, between individuals and dispositifs."[4]

Agamben and Foucault both remind us that there is no apparatus, or disposition, that does not involve the two-fold processes of subjectivation: those processes which, on one hand, "leads an individual to assume and become attached to an individuality and singularity", but on the other also leads to a "subjugation to an external power."[5] I introduce the notion of *Loving* into the Metropolitan Landscape to affect both the dynamics of subjectivation and the apparatuses that are implicated in establishing our dispositions. I suggest the philosophy of loving can counter both impulses of subjectivation: the truly loving relationship is neither too self-centred nor too compliant to the systems that establish the relations between people and between people and systems. I take the impetus from Agamben's observations on the etymology of metropolis. The term invokes the distance and relation between a mother and offspring, home and another place. The term invokes a "dishomogeneity" at the heart of our urban apparatus. The care of the mother is not that which tries to make one the same as the other. The care of the mother simply tries to make the differences between places equally loving.

In the relationship between city and landscape I promote the loving process as reciprocal; an enquiry into one should elicit love and care for the other. However, in this relation, I am neither convinced that it is the city that mothers the landscape nor the landscape that mothers the city. Alain Badiou says, "What kind of world does one see when one experiences it from the point of view of two and not one? What is the world like when it is experienced, developed and lived from the point of view of difference and not identity? This is what I believe love to be. It is the project ... from the moment our lives are challenged by the perspective of difference."[6] To elicit the

3   Ibid.
4   Ibid.
5   Ibid.
6   Alain Badiou with Nicolas Trong, *In Praise of Love*, trans. Peter Bush (London: Serpent's Tail; Profile Books, 2012) pp. 22-23.

THE [LOVING] METROPOLITAN LANDSCAPE

love and care of people together in all their differences, in all the varied dispositions between people, architecture, city and landscape, is the impetus that drives the projects illustrated in this book. The *Loving* drive does not suggest that one, either city or landscape, should be placed over the other. It moves away from the conventions of convenience that wish to compartmentalise, hold differences still and manage through categorical exclusivity. Rather, these projects and the research that drives them promote a turn towards difference, the difference that animates existence. This book illustrates the fecundity which ensues from viewing the world from a multiple rather than single perspective. Furthermore, as design-led research in the specific context of the city of Olbia in Sardinia, the Urban Design proposals raise themes and collectively inform how the loving processes might more appropriately direct the apparatuses that affect our processes for organising relations in the Metropolitan Landscape.

(DW)

L'amministrazione e l'organizzazione del nostro paesaggio sono inquadrate in paradigmi estremamente semplicistici che richiamano i concetti di bassa e alta densità. Sono modelli che stabiliscono una relazione dialettica fra le situazioni urbane e il paesaggio nella duplice versione di situazioni urbane talmente estese da racchiudere porzioni di paesaggio e quelle che, al contrario, sono meno ampie tanto da essere circondate dal paesaggio. Di solito quest'ultimo modello viene utilizzato per dare forma ai confini dell'altro. In molti paradigmi urbani massa e densità sono fattori chiave per organizzare ecologie urbane[1].

Di contro a queste tendenze riduttive è opportuno riconsiderare il paradigma territoriale sostituendo ai concetti di centro e di margine quello del bordo, inteso come condizione ri-corrente in un paesaggio continuo e aperto, un paesaggio costruito su differenti pre-occupazioni.

Per connotare con un senso di urbano le questioni del paesaggio e con un senso di paesaggio le questioni dell'urbanità ricorro al termine Metropolitan Landscape. Il [Loving] Metropolitan Landscape non sottovaluta affatto l'apporto architettonico, quello della costruzione, che geometrizza (in modo preciso e al contempo inesatto) tutte le caratteristiche del paesaggio, agrarie o urbane che siano.

Prendendo spunto da Giorgio Agamben, penso che usare il termine "metropolitano" possa designare il "nuovo tessuto urbano [e agricolo] che si viene formando parallelamente ai processi di trasformazione che Michel Foucault ha definito come passaggio dal potere territoriale dell'Ancien Régime al biopotere moderno, che è, nella sua essenza, un potere governamentale"[2].

Nel modello proposto da Agamben la relazione fra il paesaggio e l'urbano è condizionata da tre tipi di dispositivi: primo, la realtà degli esseri umani e degli altri viventi che sviluppano disposizioni fra l'uno e l'altro; secondo, dispositivi che continuamente catturano e controllano i primi; terzo, fondamentale elemento che definisce il dispositivo, è

1   Per esempio, cfr Aldo Rossi, Gli elementi primari e l'area, in Aldo Rossi (1978), L'Architettura della Città, Città Studi Edizioni, Torino, 2010
2   Giorgio Agamben, Metropolis, translated from Audio files by Arianna Bove The European Graduate School, March 17 2007, http://www.egs.edu/faculty/giorgio-agamben/articles/metropolis/. My insertion [ ].
In italiano il testo è disponibile su http://www.sinistrainrete.info/teoria/133-la-citta-e-la-metropoli.html /.[ ] è un mio inserto.

THE [LOVING] METROPOLITAN LANDSCAPE

Una serie di processi di soggettivazione che risultano dalla relazione corpo a corpo fra gli individui e i dispositivi.[3]

Agamben e Foucault ci ricordano che non esiste dispositivo o disposizione che non coinvolga duplici processi di soggettivazione. Sono processi duplici perché se da un verso permettono all'individuo di definire la propria individualità e, dunque, di caratterizzarsi nella propria singolarità, da un altro lo assoggettano a un potere esterno.

Nel Metropolitan Landscape il concetto di amore[4] richiama un elemento che connota sia le dinamiche di soggettivazione sia i dispositivi coinvolti nello stabilire le nostre disposizioni. Penso che la filosofia dell'amore possa contrapporsi a entrambi i processi di soggettivazione di cui s'è detto. La vera relazione d'amore non solo non è troppo egocentrica ma non è neanche eccessivamente compiacente verso sistemi che determinano le relazioni fra le persone e fra queste e i sistemi stessi.

Prendo spunto dall'osservazione di Agamben sull'etimologia del termine "metropoli", che evoca sia la relazione fra la madre e la sua progenie sia la distanza fra la propria dimora e un altro luogo.[5] Riferendoci al nostro apparato urbano quest'accezione ne richiama la "disomogeneità". La cura della madre, infatti, non tende a uniformare, piuttosto cerca di differenziare i luoghi pur amandoli equamente.

3   Ibid.
4   "Amore" è qui inteso come categoria filosofica, cfr oltre.
5   Etimologicamente fra la città madre e un altro suo luogo o colonia

NdT

Sono del parere che nella relazione fra città e paesaggio il processo d'amare sia un atto reciproco, una prospettiva di amore e di attenzione per l'altro. Tuttavia non sono convinto che in questo tipo di relazione la città generi il paesaggio né che il paesaggio generi la città. Alain Badiou si chiede che tipo di mondo vedremmo se lo si esperisse da due punti di vista anziché da uno solo. Come apparirebbe il mondo quando è esperito, spiegato e vissuto dal punto di vista della differenza e non dell'identità? Questo, per Badiou, è l'amore: un progetto che si avvia quando le nostre vite si devono cimentare le differenze.[6]

L'amore e la cura delle persone nelle loro differenze, nelle varie disposizioni fra loro, fra architettura, città e paesaggio, quell'amore e quella cura sono la prospettiva che attraversa i progetti presentati in questa pubblicazione. La prospettiva dell'amore fa sì che la città e il paesaggio non siano considerati antinomici né che uno dei due possa essere considerato preminente sull'altro. Si superano, in tal modo, tutte quelle consuetudini di convenienza che compartimentano e trascurano le differenze, gestendole attraverso esclusioni d'ordine categorico. In questo senso i progetti qui raccolti e la ricerca che li orienta promuovono una svolta significativa nella considerazione e nella gestione delle differenze che animano la stessa esistenza.

Vedere il mondo da un punto di vista molteplice, anziché singolo, richiama la fecondità del pensiero e, dunque, della ricerca che viene presentata in questa pubblicazione. Le proposte presentate, frutto di una ricerca-progetto effettuata nel contesto di Olbia (Sardegna), informano come il processo di amare possa essere indirizzato a dispositivi che influenzano il modo di organizzare relazioni nel Metropolitan Landscape.

(DW)

6   Alain Badiou with Nicolas Trong, *In Praise of Love*, trans. Peter Bush (London: Serpent's Tail; Profile Books, 2012) pp. 22-23.

PARA-Situation [X, Scotland]

THE (LOVING) METROPOLITAN LANDSCAPE

Architecture, Landscape and The Ecosophic Object

PARA-Situation [X, SCOTLAND]
THE [LOVING] METROPOLITAN LANDSCAPE

Architecture, Landscape and The Ecosophic Object

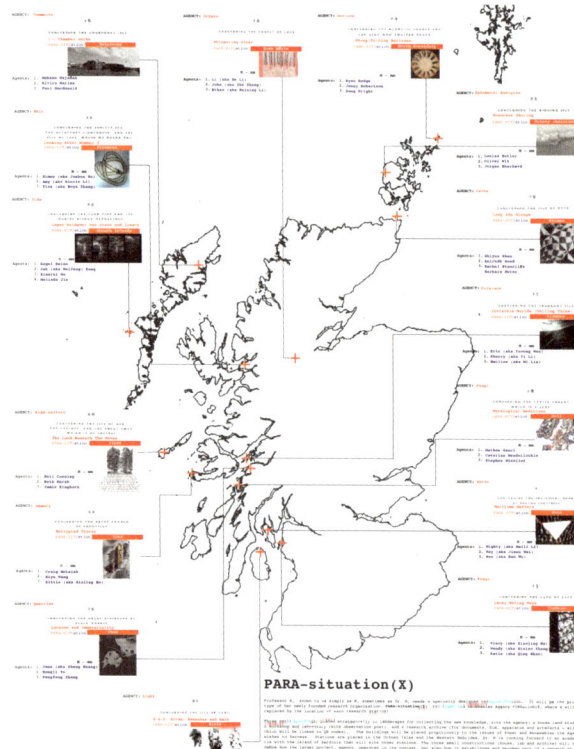

PARA-situation(X)

AGENCY: **Water**

4

CONCERNING THE EQUIVALENT BOOKS
OF DOCTOR FAUSTROLL

Maritime Matters
PARA-SITUation · **Bute**

M - mm

Agents: 1. **Mighty** (aka Maili Li)
2. **Way** (aka Jinwu Wei)
3. **How** (aka Hao Wu)

AGENCY: **Shit**

12

CONCERNING THE SQUITTY SEA,
THE OLFACTORY LIGHTHOUSE, AND THE
ISLE OF CACK, WHERE WE DRANK NOT

Looking After Number 2
PARA-SITUation · **Plockton**

M - mm

Agents: 1. **Simon** (aka Junhua Su)
2. **Amy** (aka Binxin Li)
3. **Tina** (aka Boya Zhang)

AGENCY: **Fungi**

13

CONCERNING THE LAND OF LACE

Lacey Waving Ways
PARA-SITUation · **Cumbrae**

M - mm

Agents: 1. **Vincy** (aka Xiaojing He)
2. **Wendy** (aka Sixiao Zhang)
3. **Katie** (aka Qing Shao)

ESALA

city speculations
SITUations

AGENCY: Oxygen   14

CONCERNING THE FOREST OF LOVE

Whispering Glens
PARA-SITUation   Glen Affric

M – mm

Agents: 1. Li (aka He Li)
         2. John (aka Zhe Zhang)
         3. Ethan (aka Huining Li)

AGENCY: Quarries   15

CONCERNING THE GREAT STAIRCASE OF
BLACK MARBLE
Lacunae and Immateriality
PARA-SITUation   Oban

M – mm

Agents: 1. Jane (aka Zheng Huang)
         2. Hongji Yu
         3. Pengfeng Zhang

AGENCY: Commerce   16

CONCERNING THE AMORPHOUS ISLE

(~) Chamber Works
PARA-SITUatio   Stornoway

M – mm

Agents: 1 Mohsen Najafian
         2 Elvira Marina
         3 Paul Macdonald

AGENCY: Folklore   17

CONCERNING THE FRAGRANT ISLE

Invisible Worlds (Telling Tales)
PARA-SITUation   Lismore

M – mm

Agents: 1. Eric (aka Yucong Wen)
         2. Sherry (aka Yi Li)
         3. Emiline (aka Mi Lin)

AGENCY: Fungi   18

CONCERNING THE CASTLE-ERRANT
WHICH IS A JUNK
Mycological Medicines
PARA-SITUation   Seil

M – mm

Agents: 1. Mathew Gauci
         2. Caterina Mendolicchio
         3. Stephen Micallef

AGENCY: Caves   19

CONCERNING THE ISLE OF PTYX

Loop the Gloupe
PARA-SITUation   Stroma

M – mm

Agents: 1. Shiyun Shen
         2. Anirudh Sood
         3. Rachel Stancliffe
         4. Barbara Swiec

AGENCY: Alga-culture   20

CONCERNING THE ISLE OF HER,
THE CYCLOPS, AND THE GREAT SWAN
WHICH IS OF CRYSTAL
The Land Beneath The Waves
PARA-SITUation   Tiree

M – mm

Agents: 1. Neil Cunning
         2. Ruth Marsh
         3. Jamie Kinghorn

AGENCY: Light   21

CONCERNING THE ISLE OF CYRIL

S.A.D. Arran: Sensuous and Dark
PARA-SITUation   Arran

M – mm

Agents: 1. Nia Puliyel
         2. Scott Wallace
         3. Linda Zein

AGENCY: Memory   22

CONCERNING THE GREAT CHURCH
OF SNOUTFIGS
Encrypted Traces
PARA-SITUation   Iona

M – mm

Agents: 1. Craig McLeish
         2. Siyu Wang
         3. Kittie (aka Sinling Ho)

AGENCY: Ephemeral Energies   23

CONCERNING THE RINGING ISLE

Sonorous Shoring
PARA-SITUation   Orkney (mainland)

M – mm

Agents: 1. Louisa Butler
         2. Oliver Wit
         3. Jorgen Ekerhøvd

AGENCY: Horizon   24

CONCERNING THE HERMETIC SHADES AND
THE KING WHO AWAITED DEATH
(Sheep)Folding Horizons
PARA-SITUation   North Ronaldsay

M – mm

Agents: 1. Ryan Hodge
         2. Jenny Robertson
         3. Doug Wright

AGENCY: Tide   25

CONCERNING THE LAND-TIDE AND THE
MARINE BISHOP MENDACIOUS
Lagan Bridges: sea stars and lunacy
PARA-SITUation   Monach Islands

M – mm

Agents: 1. Angel Hsiao
         2. Jak (aka Weifeng) Kong
         3. Xiaorui Ge
         4. Melinda Jin

PARA-Situation [X, SCOTLAND]

THE [LOVING] METROPOLITAN LANDSCAPE

Architecture, Landscape and The Ecosophic Object

SONOROUS SHORING

CONCERNING THE RINGING ISLE

Louisa Butler
Jørgen Ekerhovd
Oliver Wit

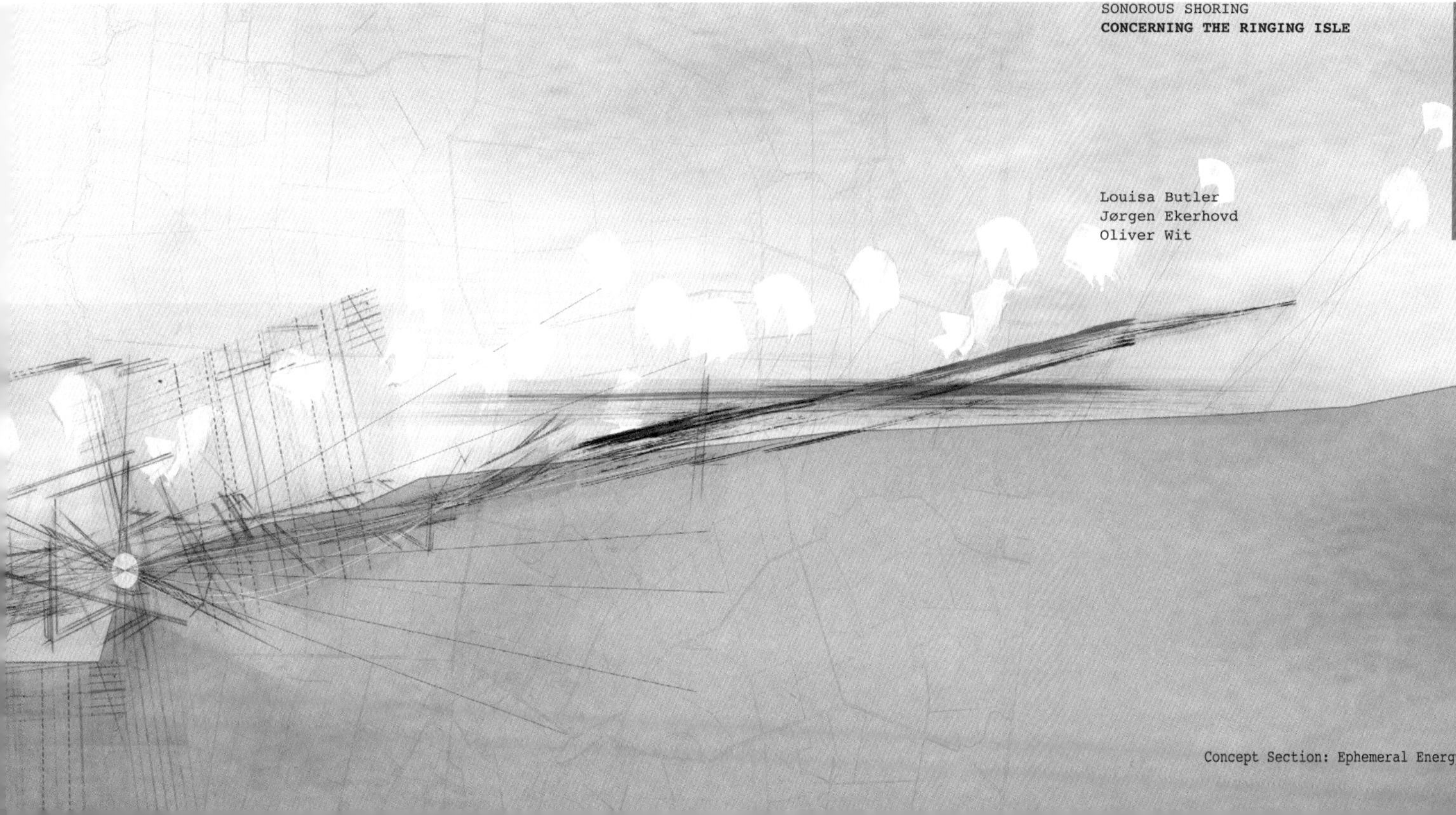

Concept Section: Ephemeral Energy

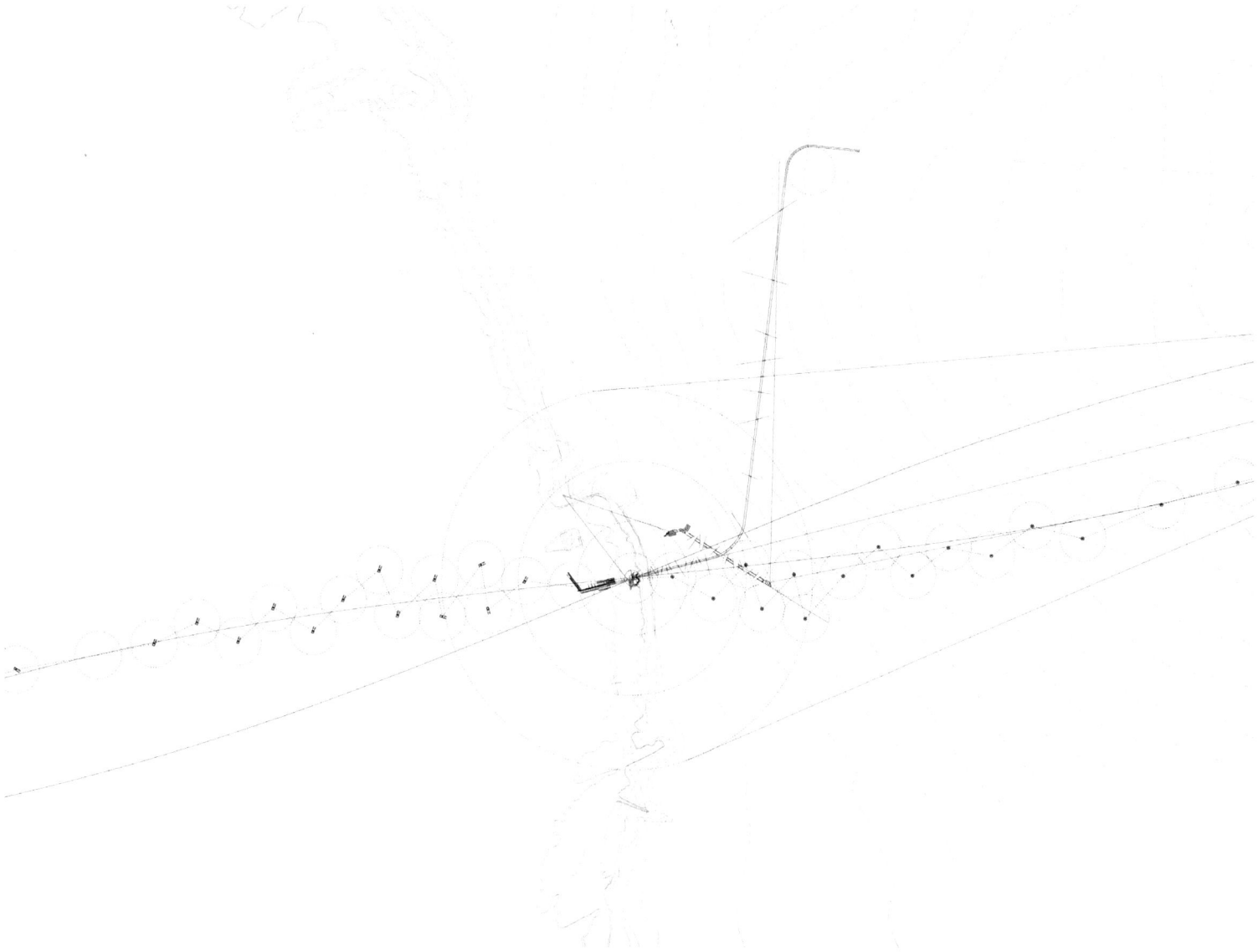

Chambers
House
Lab
Archive

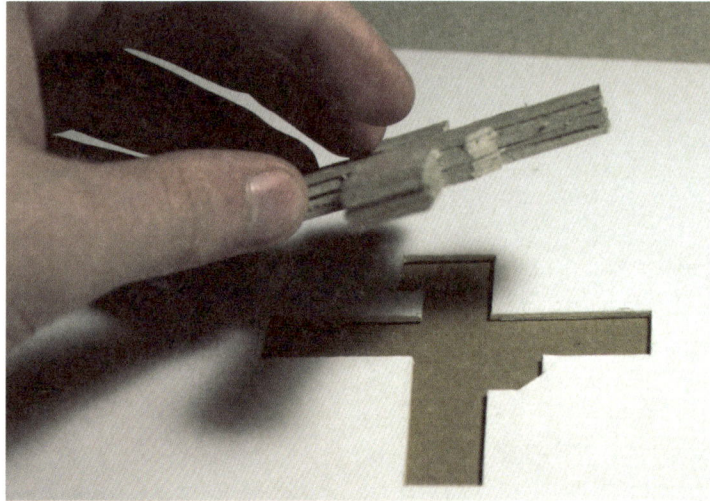

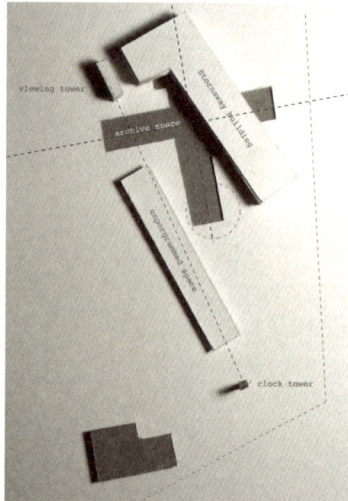

viewing tower

stairway building

archive space

suppressed space

clock tower

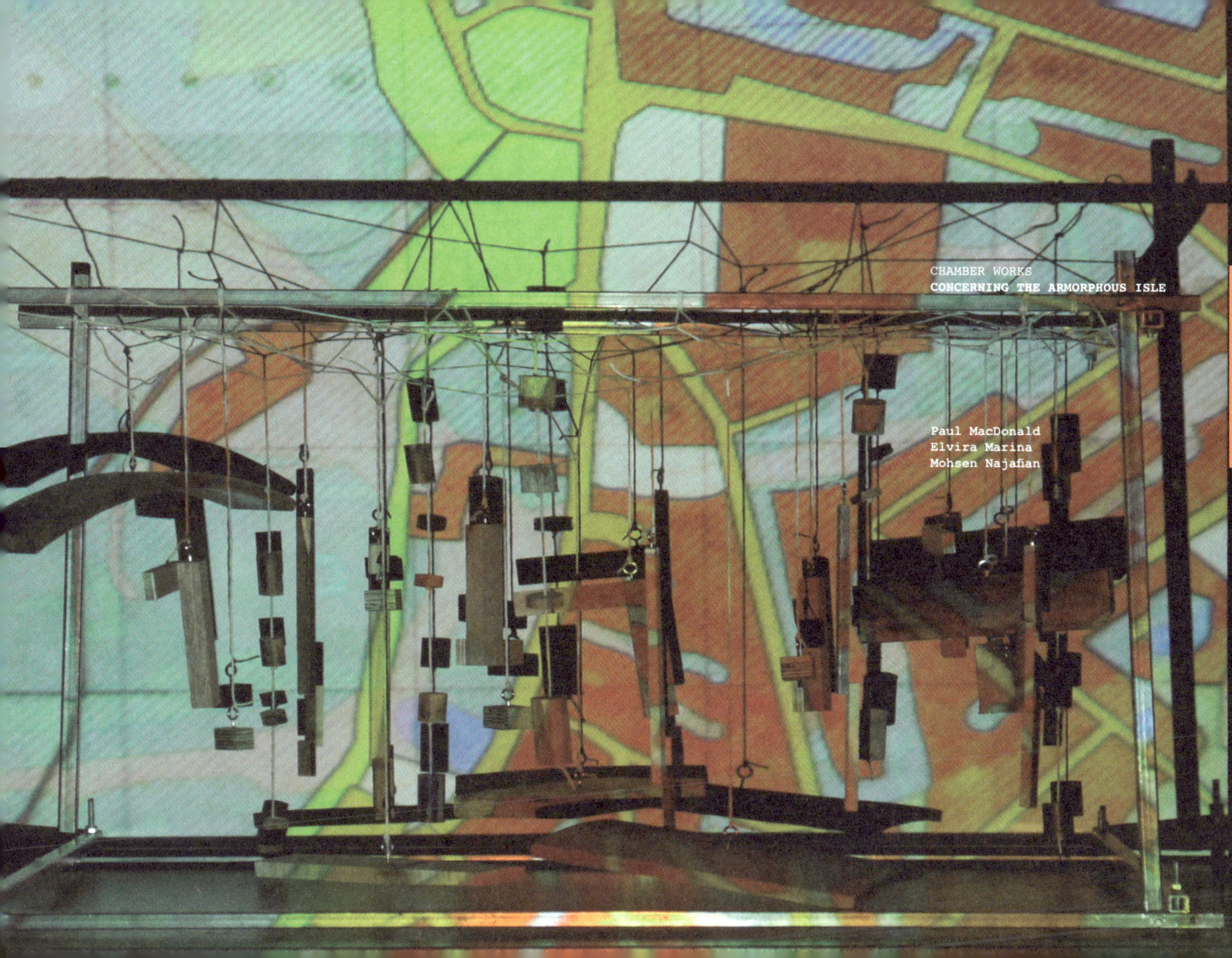

CHAMBER WORKS

CONCERNING THE ARMORPHOUS ISLE

Paul MacDonald
Elvira Marina
Mohsen Najafian

Stornaway, Lewis

Horizon
House
Lab
Archive

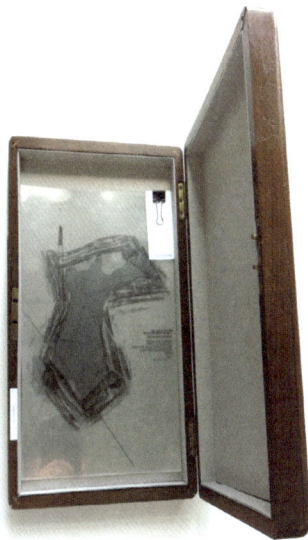

(SHEEP) FOLDING HORIZONS
**CONCERNING THE HERMETIC SHADES AND
THE KING WHO AWAITED DEATH**

Ryan J Hodge
Jennifer Robertson
Douglas J Wright

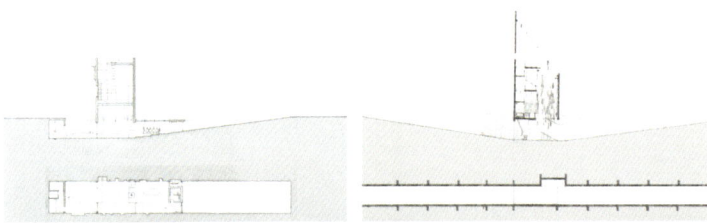
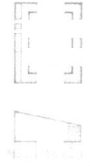

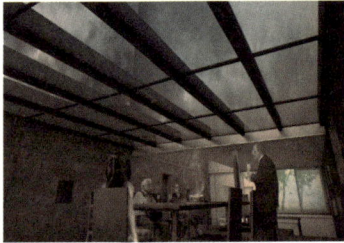

Memory
House
Lab
Archive

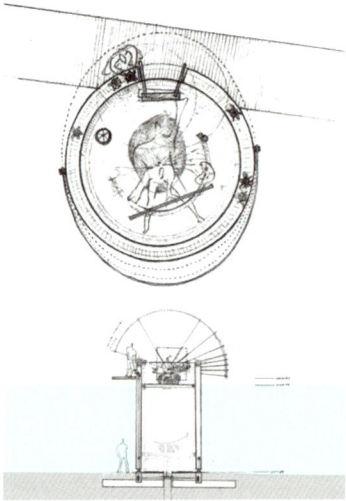

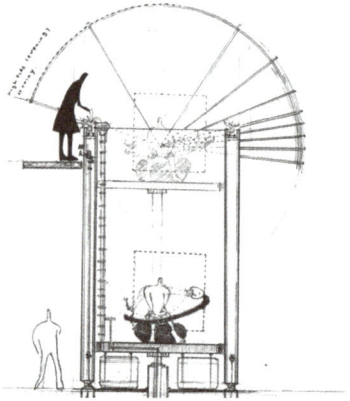

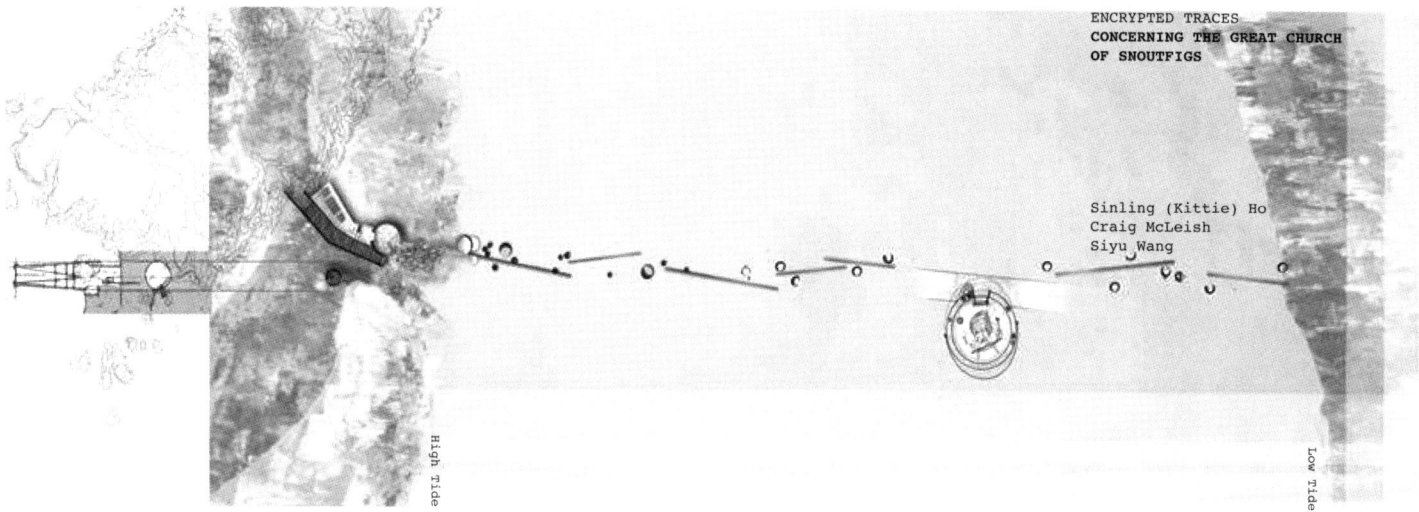

ENCRYPTED TRACES
**CONCERNING THE GREAT CHURCH
OF SNOUTFIGS**

Iona

Sinling (Kittie) Ho
Craig McLeish
Siyu Wang

High Tide

Low Tide

Algaculture
House
Lab
Archive

THE LAND BENEATH THE WAVES
CONCERNING THE ISLE OF HER, THE
CYCLOPS, AND THE GREAT SWAN WHICH
IS OF CRYSTAL

Neil Cunning
Jamie Kinghorn
Ruth Marsh

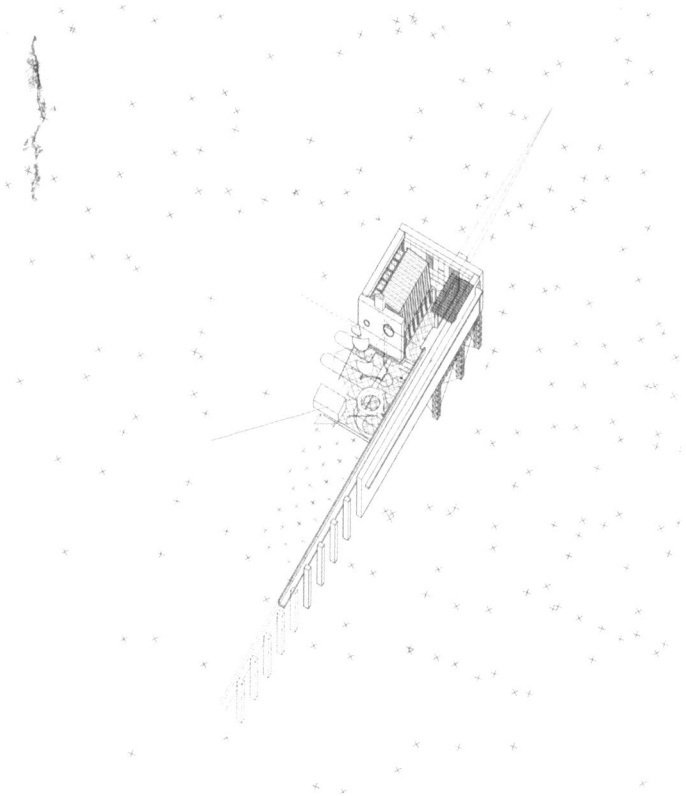

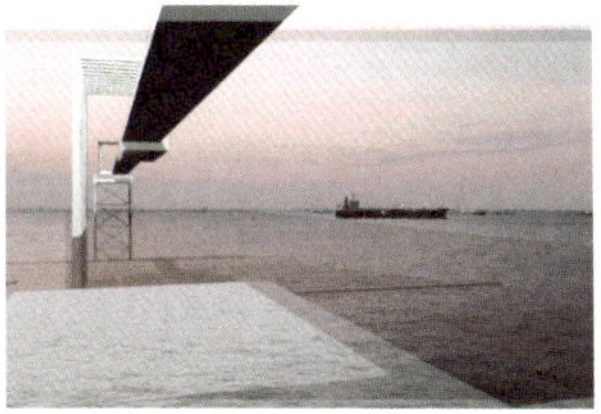

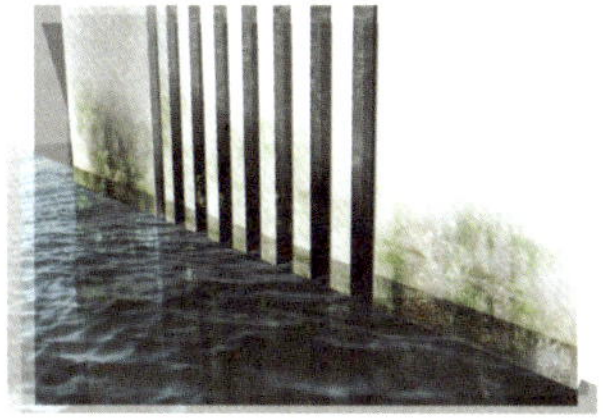

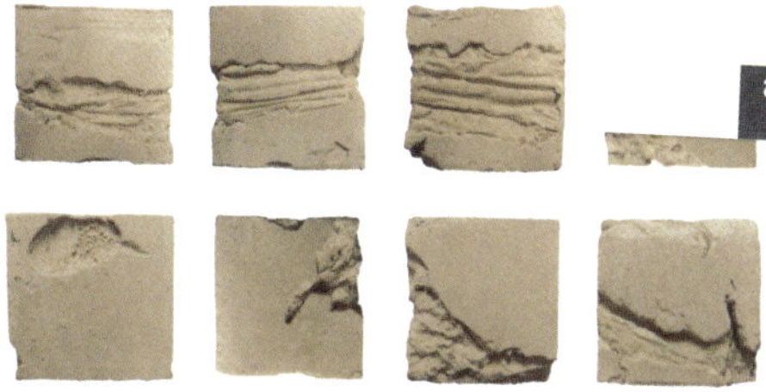

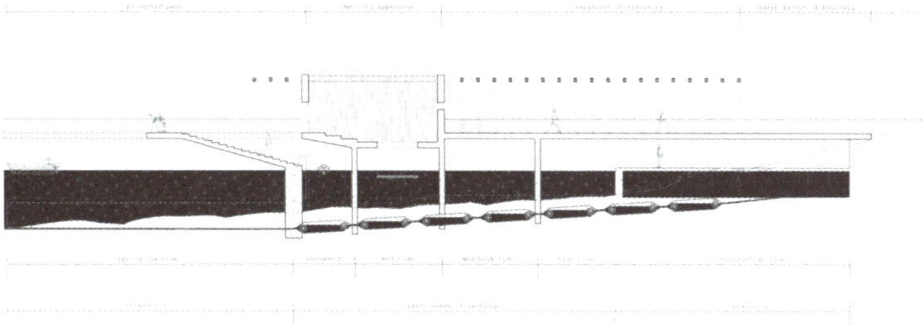

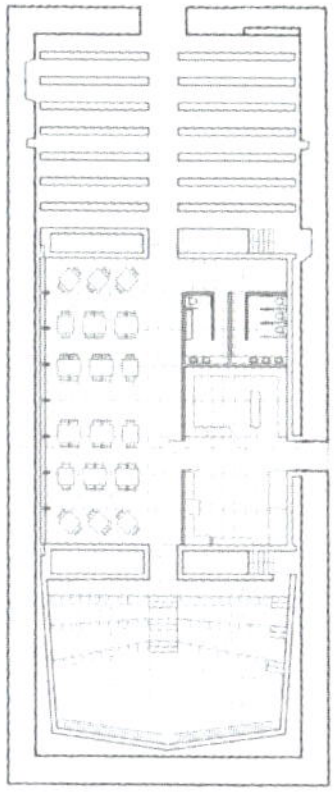

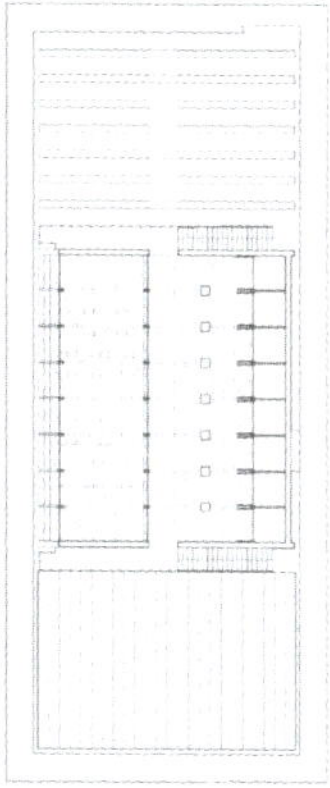

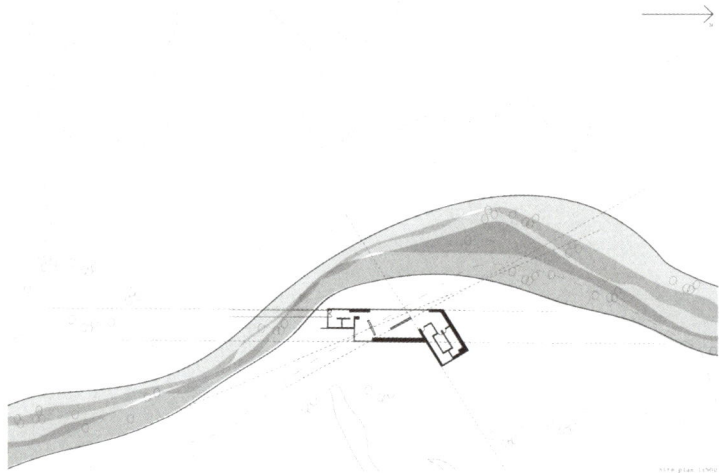

S.A.D ARRAN: SENSUOUS AND DARK
CONCERNING THE ISLE OF CYRIL

Nirupa Puliyel
Scott Wallace
Lynda Zein

Arran

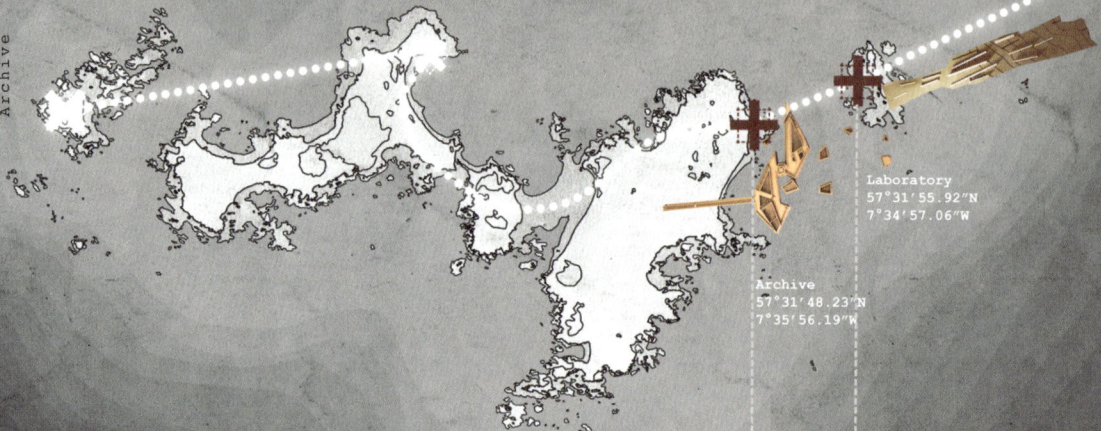

Archive
57°31'48.23"N
7°35'56.19"W

Laboratory
57°31'55.92"N
7°34'57.06"W

Station
57°34'00.83"N
7°29'15.34"W

LAGAN BRIDGES, SEA STARS AND LUNACY
CONCERNING THE LAND TIDE AND THE
MARINE BISHOP MENDACIOUS

Weifeng (Jack) Kong
Zhwen Hsiao
Xiaohui C.
Weizhda Jin

House
57°33'03.64"N
7°22'38.78"W

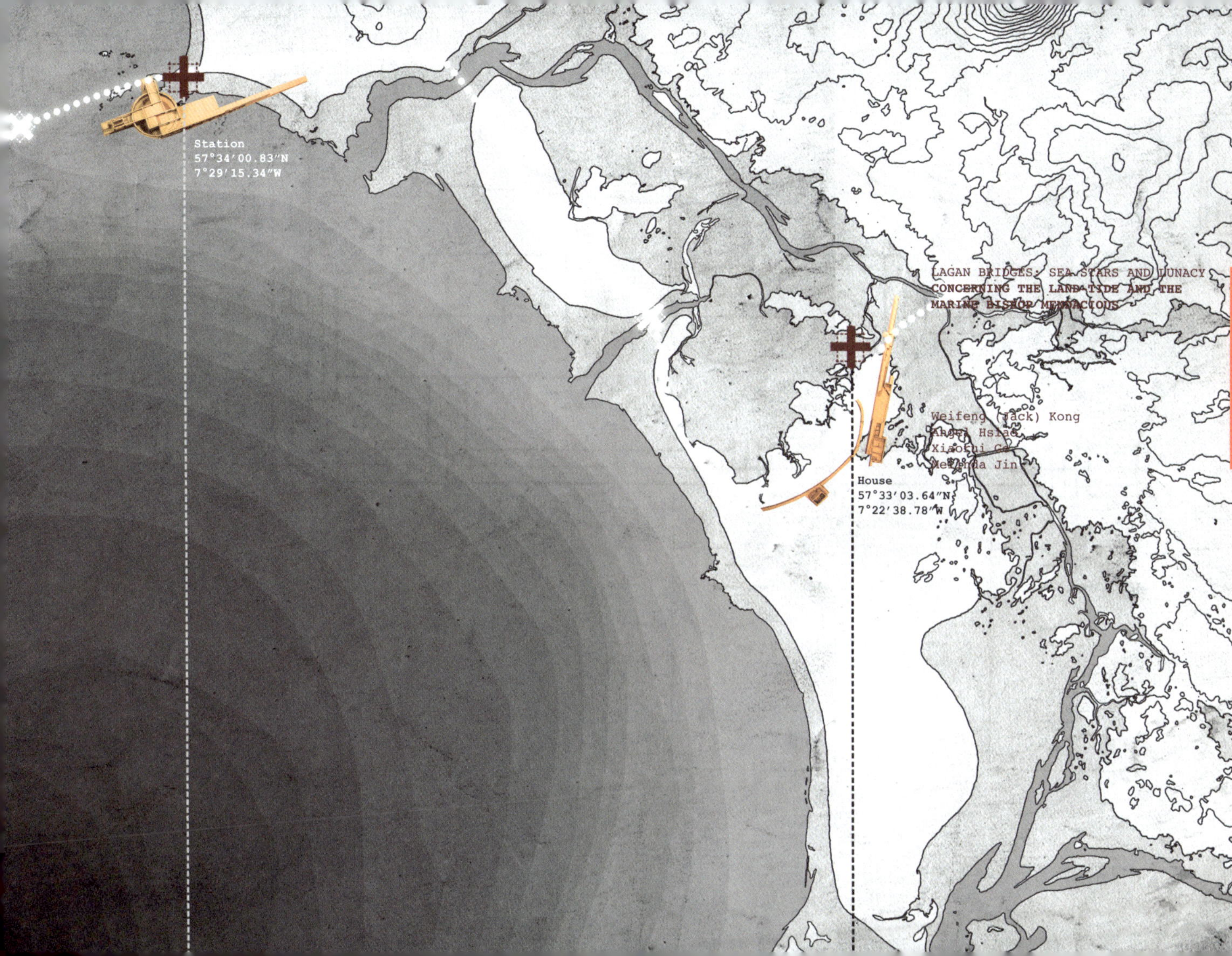

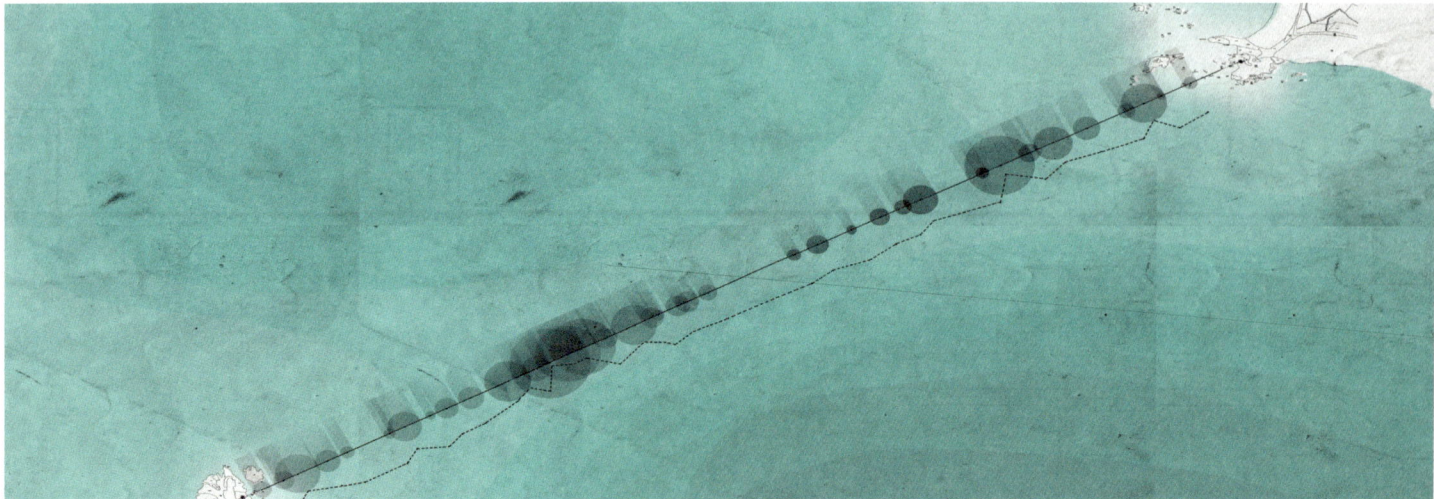

Medicine
House
Lab
Archive

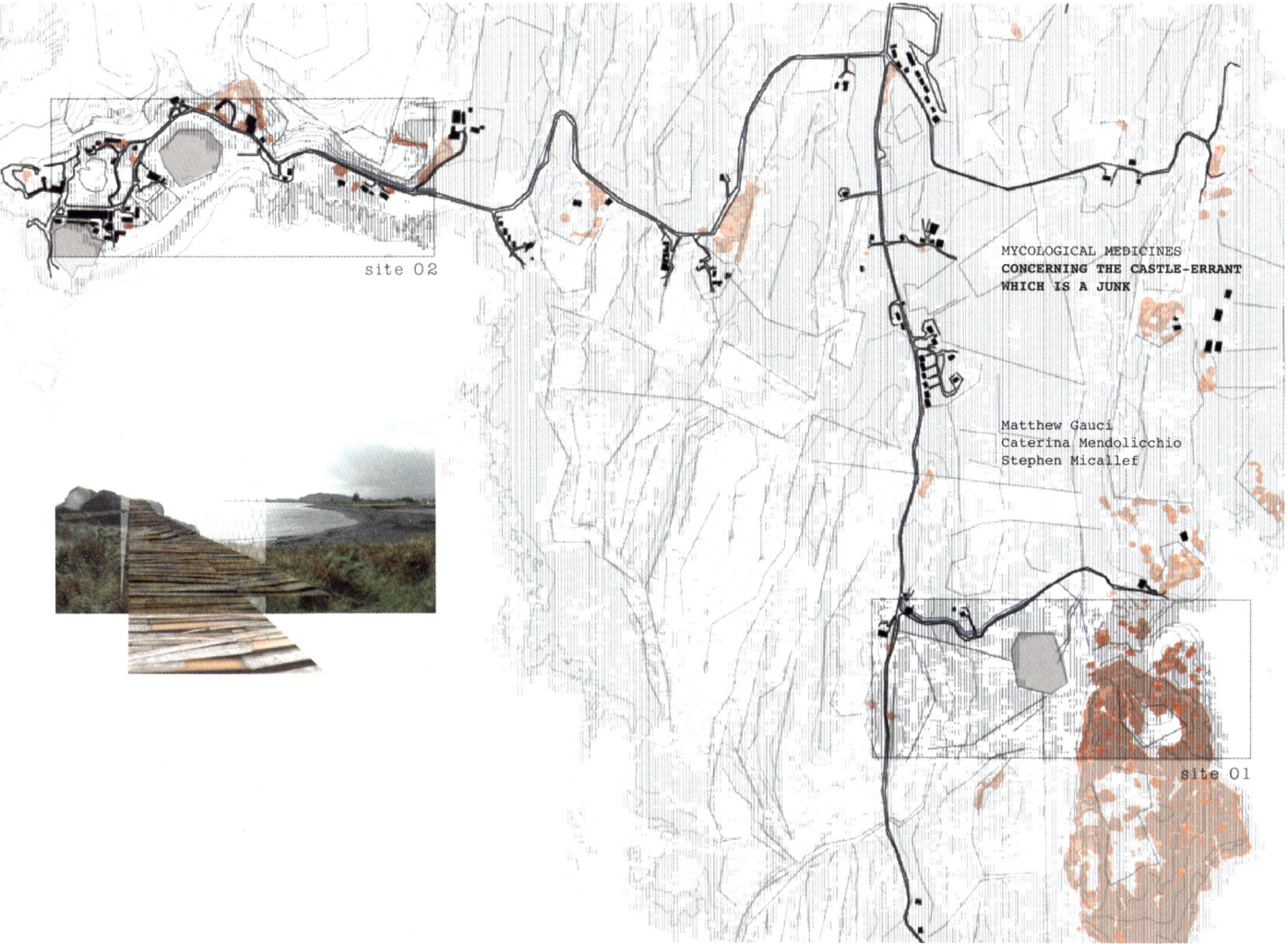

site 02

MYCOLOGICAL MEDICINES
CONCERNING THE CASTLE-ERRANT
WHICH IS A JUNK

Matthew Gauci
Caterina Mendolicchio
Stephen Micallef

site 01

seil

Caves
House
Lab
Archive

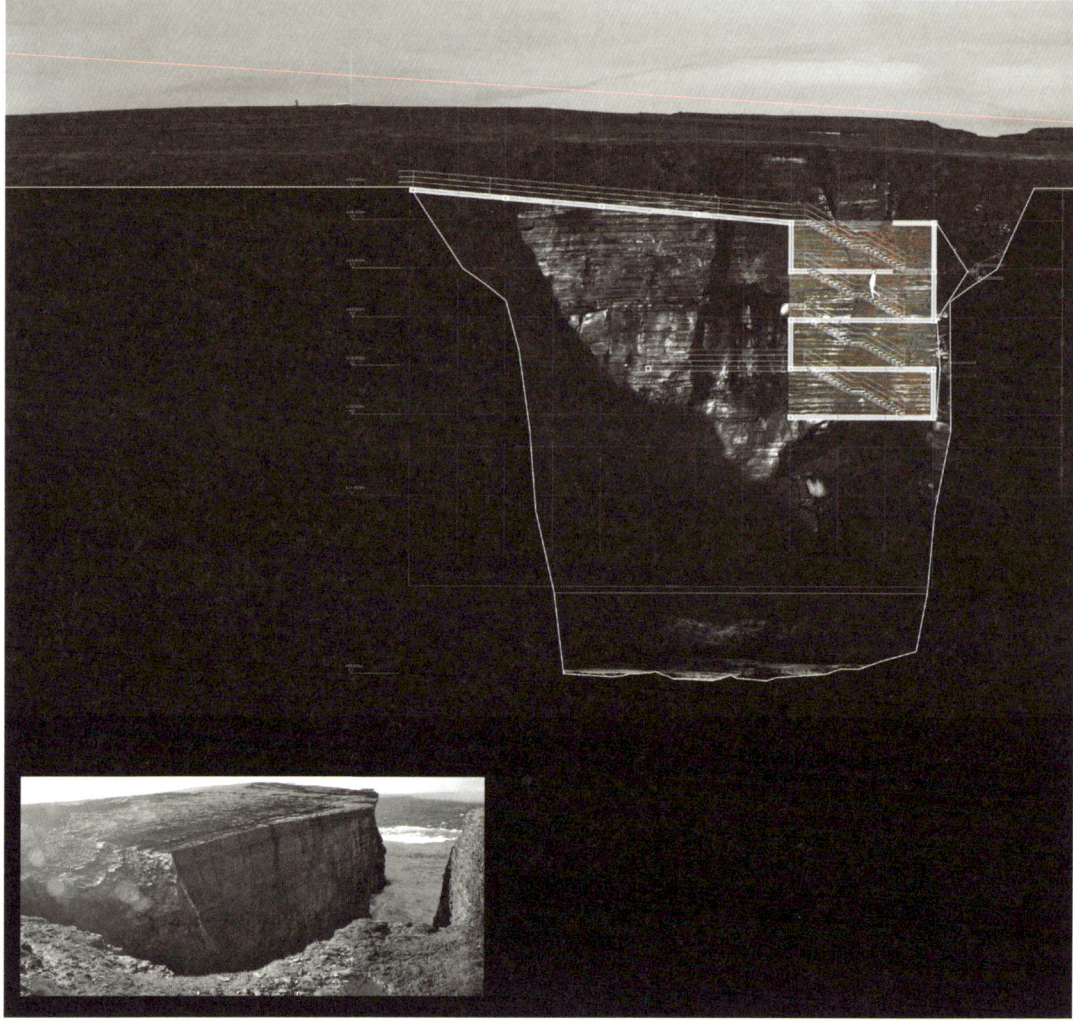

LOOP THE GLOUPE
CONCERNING THE ISLE OF PTYX

Shiyun (Sharon) Shen
Anirudh Sood
Rachel Stancliffe
Barbara Swierc

PARA-Situation [X]
THE [LOVING] METROPOLITAN LANDSCAPE
Architettura, Paesaggio e L'oggetto Ecosofico

Facoltà di Architettura
Università degli Studi di Sassari

WORKSHOP

3-12 novembre 2011
Asilo Sella, Lungomare Garibaldi, Alghero

ARCHITECTURE, LANDSCAPE & THE ECOSOPHIC OBJECT

Facoltà di Architettura
Università degli Studi di Sassari

8 novembre 2011 ore 18.30
Aula Magna
Asilo Sella, Lungomare Garibaldi, Alghero

Conferenza
Dorian Wiszniewski

MUD, DISPOSITION, SITUATION AND PARASITUATION

The paper will principally call upon the writings of Michel Serres and Giorgio Agamben, in particular how they each develop the "paradigmatic character" and how this "beside ways" thinking extends geographical horizons. The paper works in the metaphorical abundance of mud (and loam), articulates disposition through Agamben's critical understanding of architecture and geography as apparatuses and considers situation through Serre's notion of the parasite, or as I call it here, the para-situation.

Dorian Wiszniewski is Senior Lecturer in Architectural Design and Theory, ESALA, University of Edinburgh. Since joining University of Edinburgh in 1996, he has taught at various UG and PG levels and on every level of the professionally accredited Architecture programmes. Research interests, which directly correspond to taught courses, concern design practice as incited by the languages of theoretical critique. He is currently Programme Director for the following PG Programmes: PhD by Design, Master of Architecture Integrated Pathway, M.Sc Architectural and Urban Design, M.Sc Reflective Design Practices.

A

SEMINARIO DELLA SCUOLA DI DOTTORATO
Giovedì 10 novembre 2011 ore 10.00 | Stabilimento Lido (mensa universitaria)

prof. Dorian Wiszniewski ESALA Edinburgh

incontra i dottorandi:

The sustainable future of the low density city Giovanni Maria Biddas

Urban quality of life Giovanna Fancello

Architecture | Mental Health | Society Giuliana Frau

Public space as a dispositif? Francesca Rango

The urban territory Michele Valentino

Facoltà di Architettura
Università degli Studi di Sassari

A

Silvia Lai, Mario Quneddu, Sara Manriega, Fabio Campus, Dario Cocco, Mariella Musalà, Nora Ondrusko, Giuseppe Zingaro, Antonio Secundo, Samuaina Diana, Baldassare Pio, Davide Secchi, Daniele Ruiu, Salvatore Cambiargiu, Margherita Ferrest, Giovanni Ortu, Alessandra Crobeddu, Anna Coccuccu, Sana Fadda, He Lu, Zhe Zhang, Hunning Lu, Craig McLeish, Sian Wang, Seiting Ho, Neil Cumming, Ruth March, Irene Kingdom, Illa Pollard, Scott Wallace, Landre Zein, Matthew Gucci, Caterina Mendola, Clou, Stephan Minz-altel, Louisa Butler, Oliver Wa, Jorgen Eemhault, Yuczing Wen, H.U. Mi Loo, Jalka Weifeng, Kong, Xaorou Lai, Melinda, on, Stiijean Sliem, Anirudh Snod, Rachel Spicciffc, Barbara Siraer, Ryan Hodge, Kristy Robert, son, Dovig Wright, Motham Nayafari, Elena Medina, Paul Macdonald, Zheng Huaing, Pengfeng Zhang, Jinwu Wei, Han Wu, Angar Huan

Dorian Wiszniewski, Kevin Adams, Karl Nurmini, Silva Serreli, Samantta Bartocci, Verdina Satta, Cristian Cannaos, Giovanni Maria Biddau, Elio Bedunda

PRESENT THEIR WORK
Venerdì 11 | 11 | 2011 ore 16.30

Aula Conferenza Liceo Classico
via Carlo Alberto 92
Alghero

ARCHITECTURE,
LANDSCAPE & THE ECOSOPHIC OBJECT

Facoltà di Architettura
Università degli Studi di Sassari

PARA-Situation [X, OLBIA, Sardinia]

THE (LOVING) METROPOLITAN LANDSCAPE

Architecture, Landscape and The Ecosophic Object

THE [LOVING] METROPOLITAN LANDSCAPE

Architecture, Landscape and The Ecosophic Object

Each context is in possession of its own peculiarity as a construction of elements in time: the historical instances, the morphology, the knowledge and the relation among those (and much more). These peculiarities constitute a territory. Frequently designing means the setting of a series of devices which take into account the context, and which are, at the same time, an alteration. Such alterations in order to build or open new realities.

La peculiarità di ogni contesto è una costruzione nel tempo: le istanze storiche, i saperi, la morfologia nonché la relazione fra tutti questi elementi (e molti altri) fanno un territorio. Ogni territorio presenta le sue peculiarità e, di solito, progettare significa predisporre dispositivi che tengano conto dei contesti ma che, allo stesso tempo, ne propongono un'alterazione per costruire o avviare una nuova realtà.

On the other hand, in the globalized world, according to a market perspective, seeking for peculiarity frequently leads to the paradox of homogenisation of the urban landscape, generalising some places to be similarly different from other places. As Harvey[1] remarks, the market needs the peculiarity of places to expand (for example for tourism), but through the single perspective of commodification, it destroys the uniqueness needed to feed itself.

In ottica di mercato, però, la ricerca della peculiarità produce paesaggi urbani omologati, che paradossalmente si presentano differenti in un modo simile. Come ricorda

1   David Harvey, The Art of Rent: Globalization, Monopoly and the commodification of culture, in http://www.16beavergroup.org/mtarchive/archives/001966.php

Harvey[2], l'economia cerca la peculiarità del luogo (si pensi al turismo) ma, proponendo un punto di vista unico, quello dello sfruttamento economico appunto, distrugge l'unicità del territorio di cui cercava di alimentarsi.

Sardinia is not beyond the economic processes of the global scale, but, rather than being a propeller, it is a land partially affected by trends elsewhere. As such, its land is dotted with small towns, which have lost their urban quality of life. Mindful of past social, economic and settlement structures, they are places that deserve to open towards urban perspectives different from the one proposed by economic inanity.

La Sardegna non può sottrarsi dai processi economici a scala globale, ma non ne è sicuramente un attore principale. Piuttosto, in molti casi, è un territorio che risente degli andamenti di quei processi e, come tale, oggi si presenta costellato da piccoli centri che hanno perso una specifica qualità della vita urbana, tanto che le memorie di strutture insediative, sociali ed economiche del passato che necessitano di una rilettura, in chiave contemporanea, per aprirsi a una prospettiva urbana diversa da quella prettamente economica.

The focus of the design and research process of this work is the city of Olbia and the coastal territory of Gallura. Olbia, the core of the North-East of Sardinia, shows the presence of some important infrastructures - the port and airport - and the transformations generated by the expansion of tourist settlement. In contrast to other cities of Sardinia, here the population is rapidly increasing. Because of its peculiarities, the city needs a reflection able to valorize and to link its settlement system to the environment.

Questi lavori, ricerca e progetto, si sono concentrati in modo particolare sulla città di Olbia e sul territorio costiero della Gallura. Olbia, centro cardine del territorio nord-orientale della Sardegna, vede la presenza di fondamentali infrastrutture - porto e aeroporto - e di trasformazioni insediative generate dall'espansione turistica. Contrariamente al resto delle grandi città sarde è una città che si espande e che vede crescere rapidamente la sua popolazione. Proprio per

2   David Harvey, The Art of Rent: Globalization, Monopoly and the commodification of culture, in http://www.16beavergroup.org/mtarchive/archives/001966.php

queste sue peculiarità necessità di una riflessione progettuale che sia capace di dare valore e di legare il suo sistema insediativo a quello ambientale.

This works offers twofold richness. First, it is a work of de-construction, an act of knowledge that lays bare the territory; secondly it is a re-construction that aggregates multiple gazes exploring its potential.

Alcune di queste riflessioni sono alla base della ricerca degli studenti dell' ESALA che ci offrono un lavoro duplicemente ricco. É un lavoro di de-costruzione, un atto di conoscenza che "denuda" il territorio e ne propone una ri-costruzione in grado di unire sguardi molteplici e di indagarne le potenzialità.

"We live in the best of all possible worlds." Seemingly going along with Voltaire's Candide, taking issue with Leibniz and Panglossian fixity, this work on Olbia suggests the possibility of different worlds, that is, design scenarios that do not simply reinforce the existing structures of the world but which operate to emergent and urgently important political, philosophical and ecosophic values.

"Viviamo nel migliore dei mondi possibili": in qualche modo memore della critica del Candido di Voltaire a Leibniz e alla fissità di Pangloss, questo lavoro su Olbia suggerisce la possibilità di mondi differenti, ossia scenari che non si limitano a rinforzare le strutture esistenti, ma operano su valori politici, filosofici ed ecosofici emergenti.

(FR)
(MV)

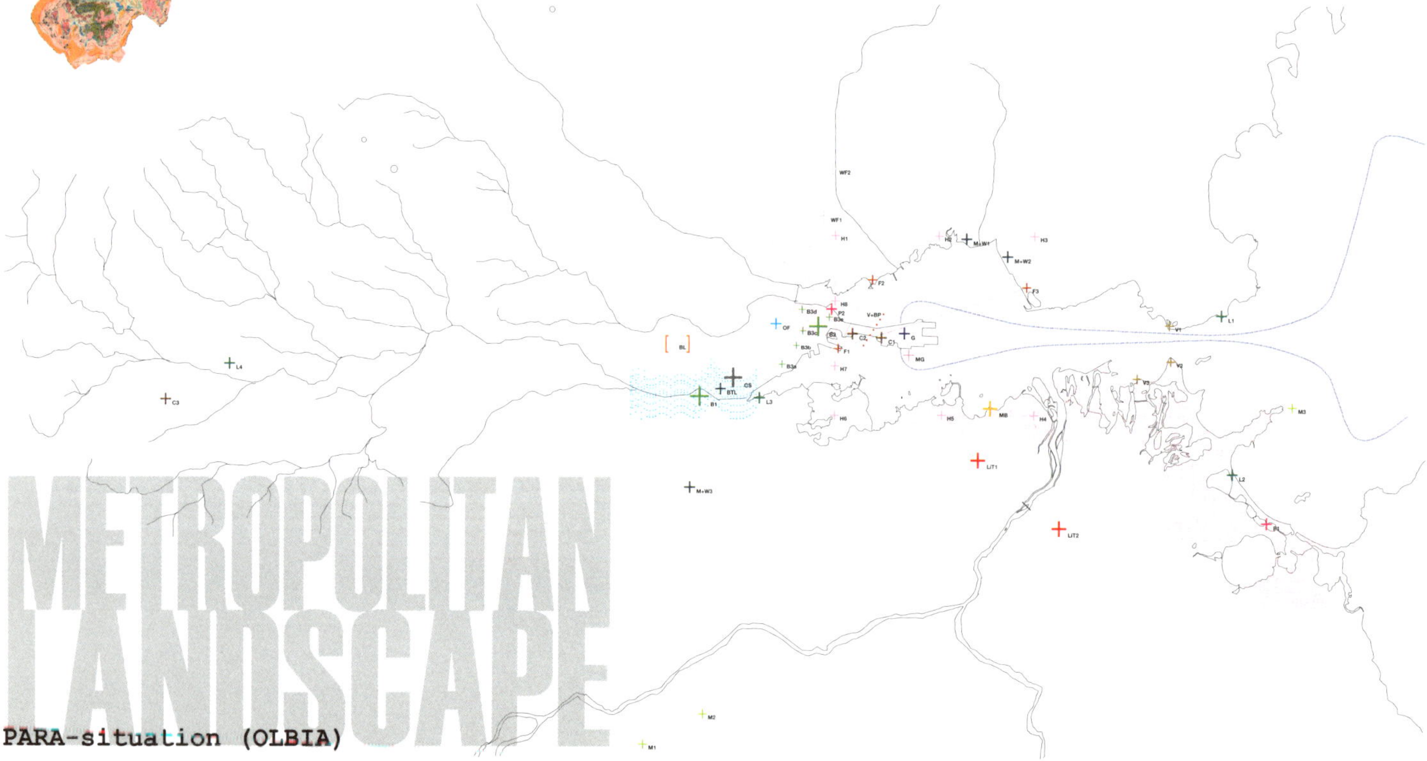

METROPOLITAN
LANDSCAPE

PARA-situation (OLBIA)

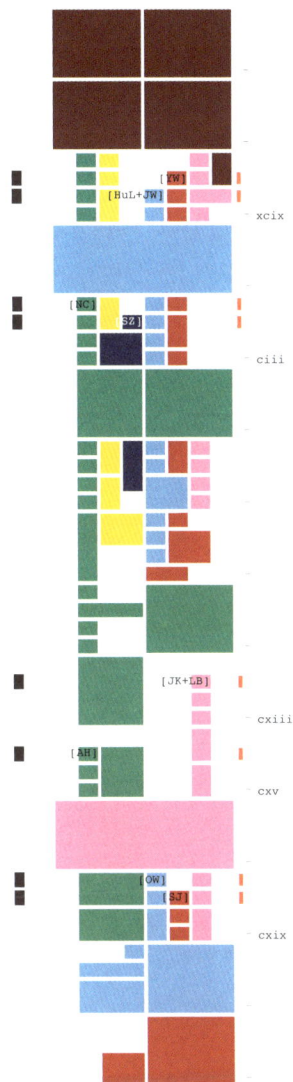

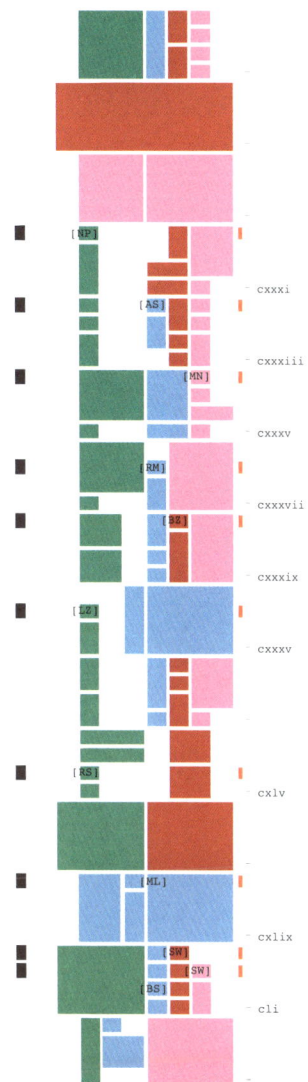

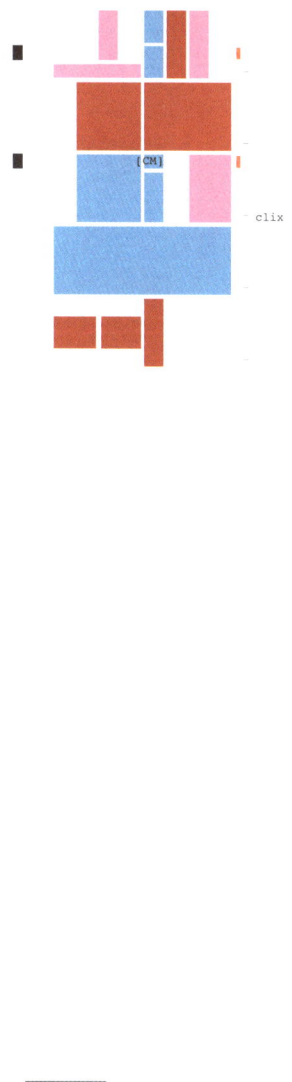

[PH]
[SH]
[RH+DJW]
[MG+SM+ZZ]

lxv

[PZ+HL+ZH+HW]
[LM]

lxix

[LB]

lxxv

WK+SS+MJ

lxxix

[YL]
[JE]
[QS]

lxxxvii

[JR]

lxxxix

[FW]
[HuL+JW]

xcix

[NC]
[SZ]

ciii

[JK+LB]

cxiii

[AH]

cxv

[OW]
[SJ]

cxix

[NP]

cxxxi

[AS]

cxxxiii

[MN]

cxxxv

[RM]

cxxxvii

[SS]

cxxxix

[LZ]

cxxxv

[RS]

cxlv

[ML]

cxlix

[SW]
[SW]
[BS]

cli

[CM]

clix

[BZ]

[MN]

[SVH]

[MJ]

[SH]

[RH]

[SH]

[SH]

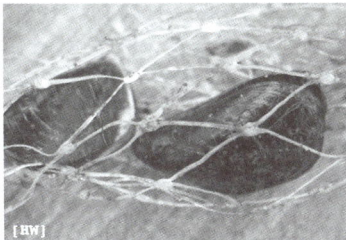

[HW]

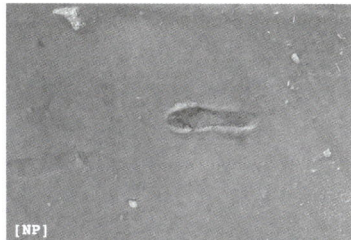

[NP]

[SH]

[MN]

[BZ]

[SH]

[NP]

[OW]

[NP]

THE [LOVING] METROPOLITAN LANDSCAPE

Architecture, Landscape and The Ecosophic Object

Saints Sinners
Medical School

The Humors
Housing
Workshops
Civic Halls
Boating
Sailing
Harbour

Minerality
Paint-works
Salt-works
Osmos Plant
House
Pawn Shop

Exchange
Housing Quay
Master's House
Workshop
Museum

SALT LINES AND OLBIAN
LAMPREY: TABLES OF OLBIA

Ryan J. Hodge
Douglas J. Wright

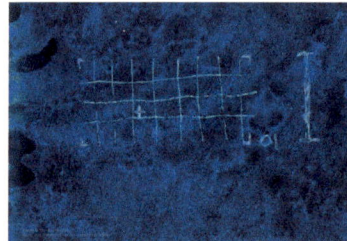

EDGE CONTINUITY

Matthew Gauci
Stephen Micalief
(John) Zhe Zhang

LOST IN TRANSLATION:
SCHOOL OF MEDICINE

Paul MacDonald

VINEGAR AND BROWN PAPER:
ISOLA BIANCA AND URBAN EDGES

(Kittie) Sinling Ho

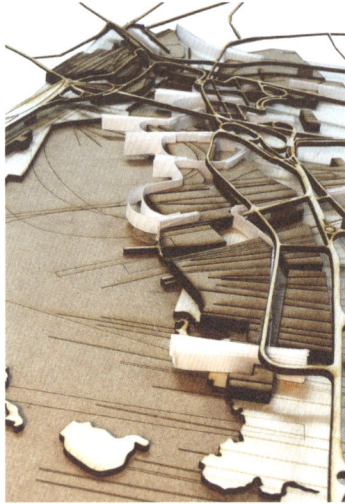

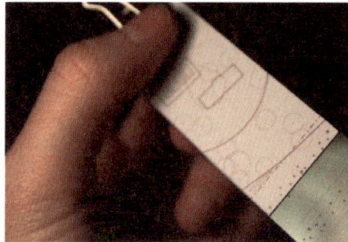

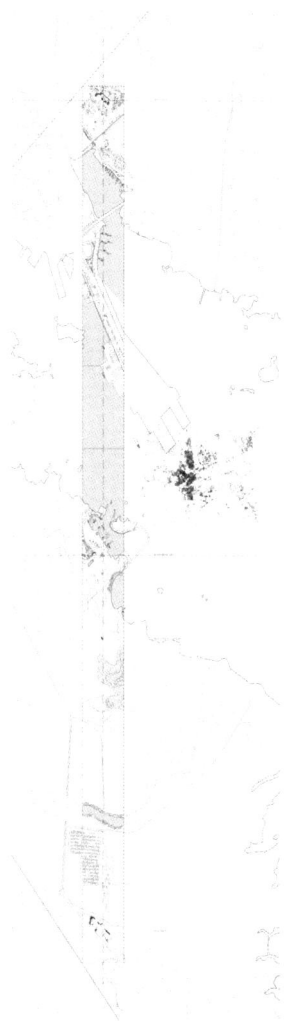

1682mm

Gastronomy
Delight
Connection

Cork
Cheese
Wine
Mussels
Sport
Resturants
Filtration

Event
Spontaneity
Play

Museum
Resturant
Park
Civic Hall

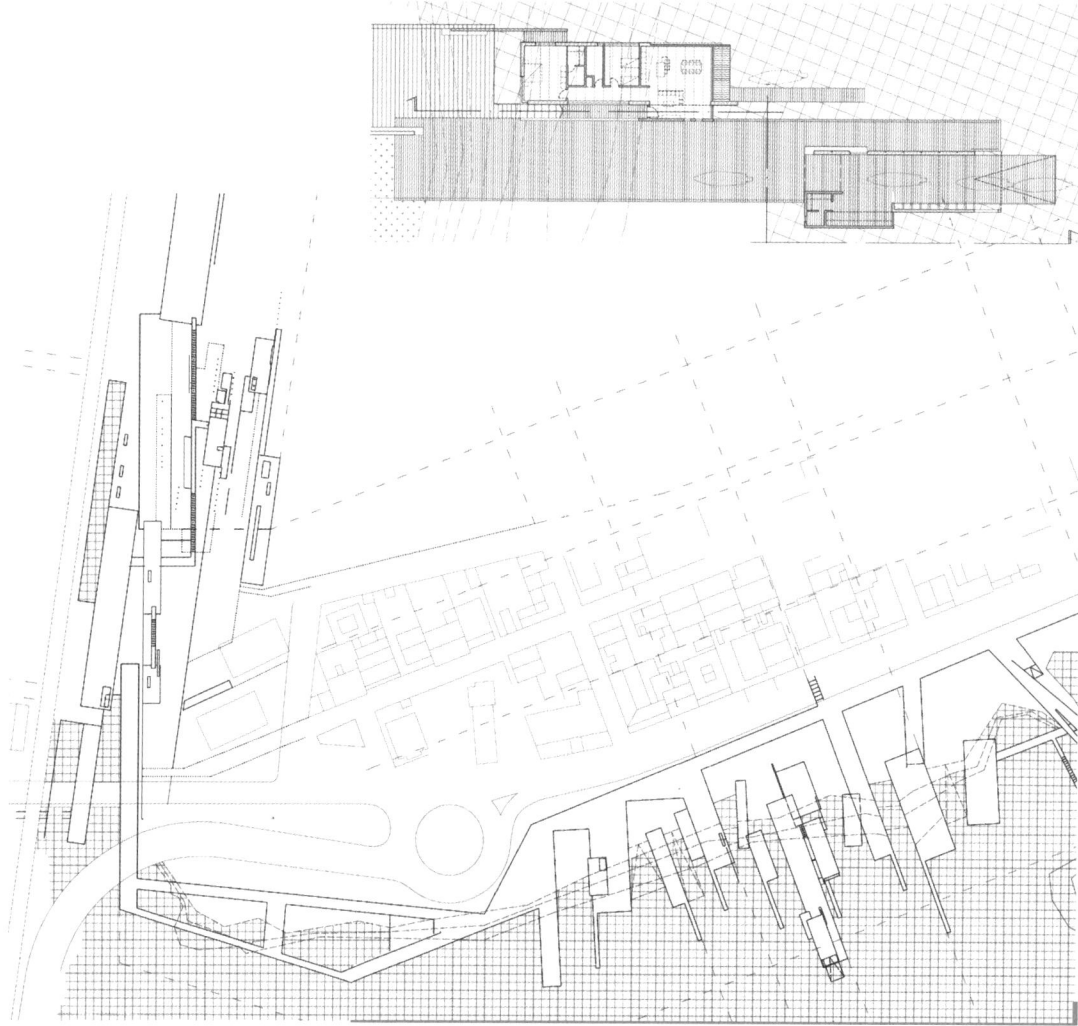

BRIDGING GUILDS

Zhang Pengfeng
Li He
(Jane) Huen Zheng
(How) Wu Hao

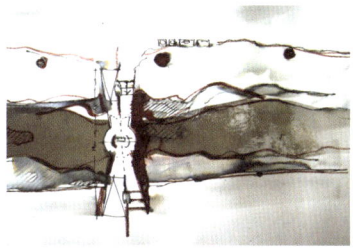

FUN PALACE

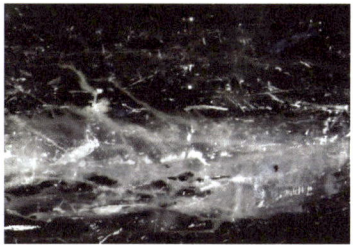

(Mighty) Li Maili

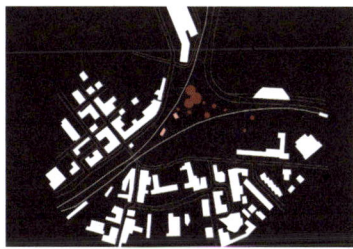

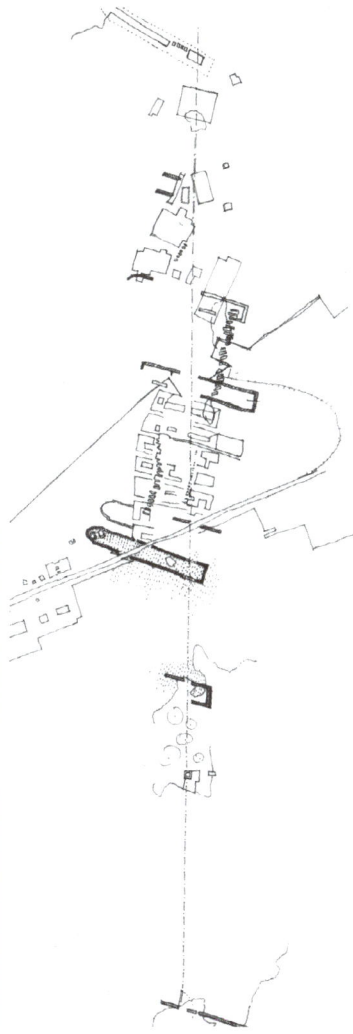

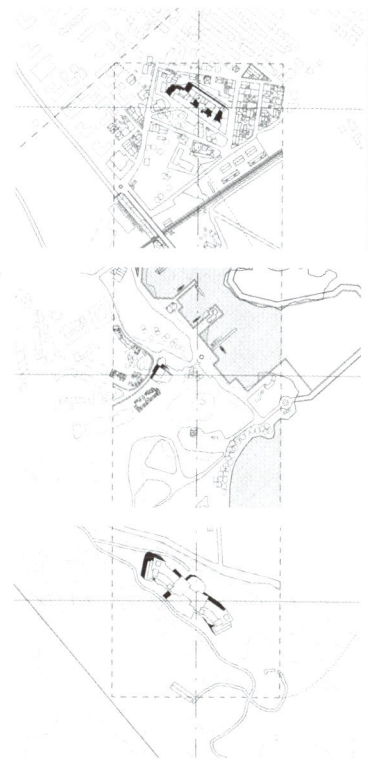

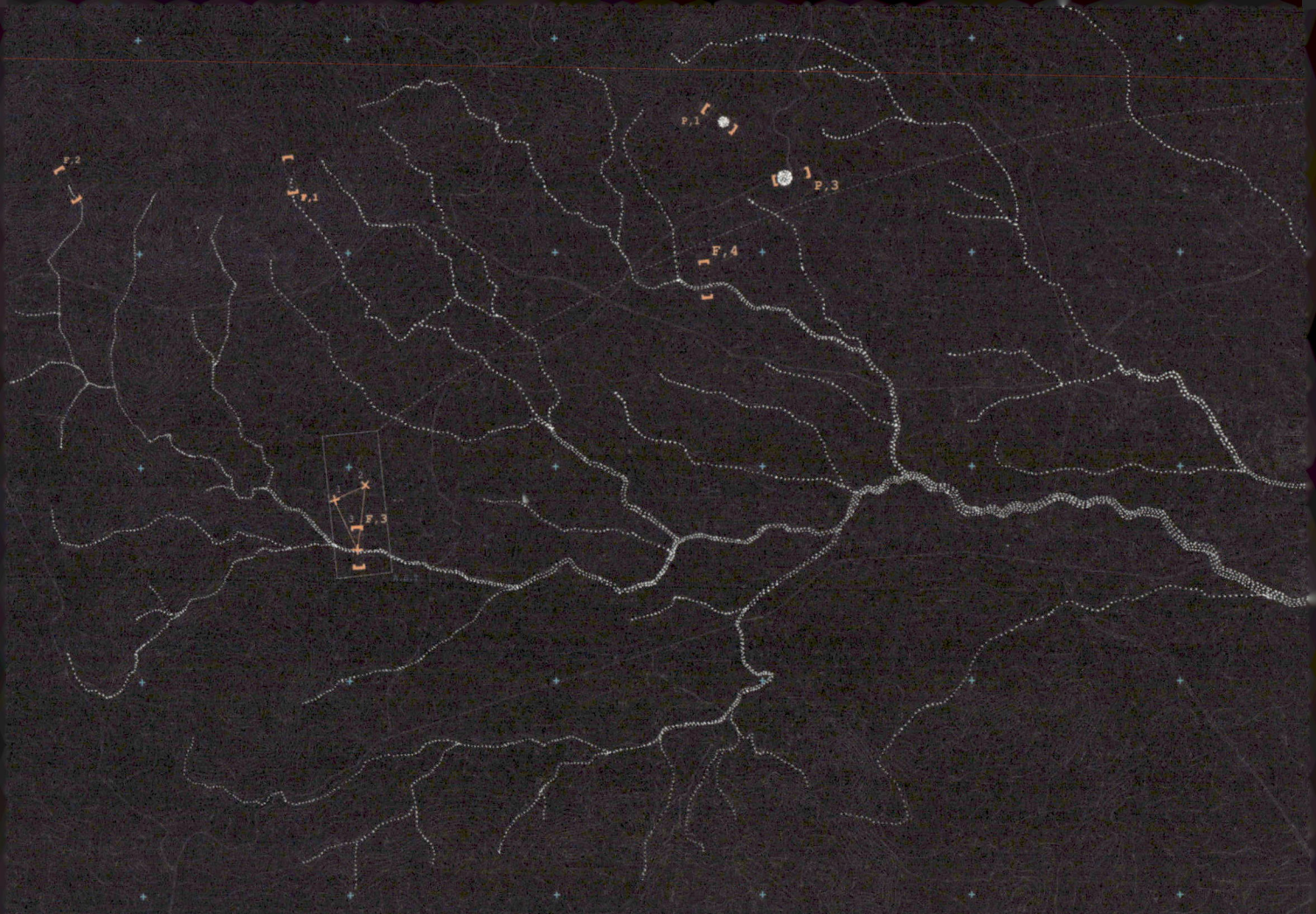

P.1

F.2

F.1

P.3

F.4

1 2 ✕
3 F.3

Mapping the Saline Territories of Olbia

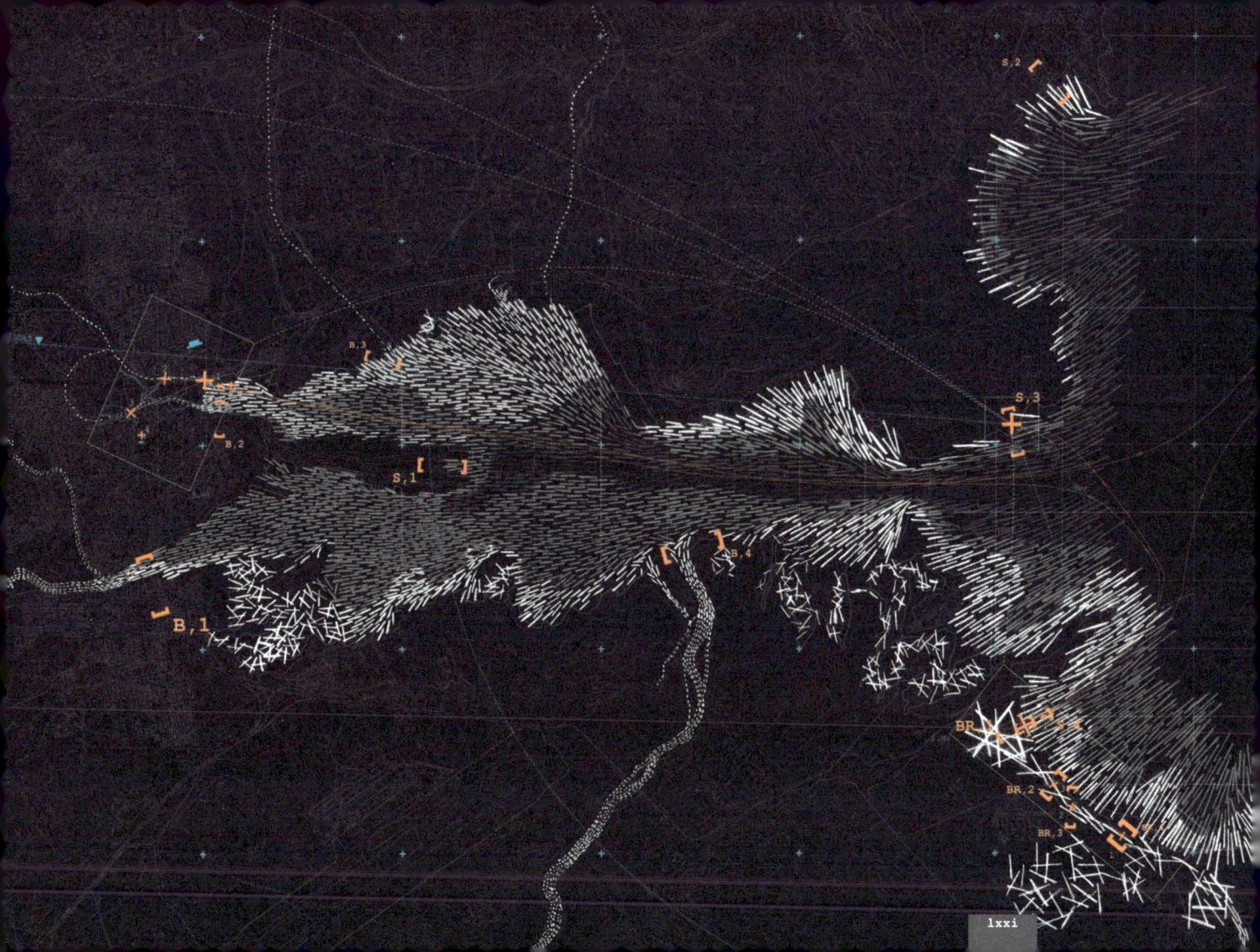

S,2

B,3

S,3

S,1

B,2

B,4

B,1

BR,1
S,4

BR,2

BR,3

lxxi

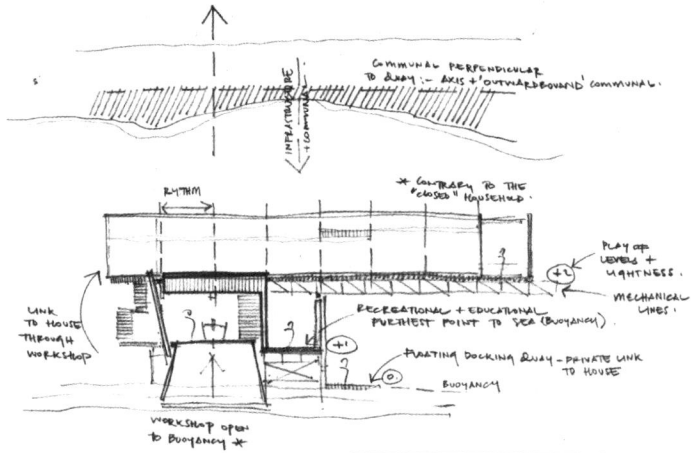

COMMUNAL PERPENDICULAR
TO QUAY :- AXIS + 'OUTWARD BOUND' COMMUNAL.

INFRASTRUCTURE
+ COMMUNAL

S

RYTHM

* CONTRARY TO THE
"CLOSED" HOUSEHOLD.

+2

PLAY OF
LEVELS +
LIGHTNESS.

MECHANICAL
LINES.

LINK
TO HOUSE
THROUGH
WORKSHOP

RECREATIONAL + EDUCATIONAL
FURTHEST POINT TO SEA (BUOYANCY).

+1

FLOATING DOCKING QUAY - PRIVATE LINK
TO HOUSE

BUOYANCY

WORKSHOP OPEN
TO BUOYANCY *

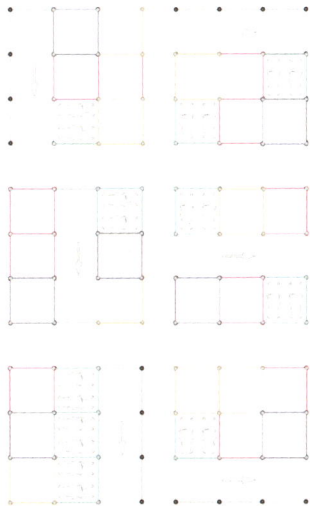

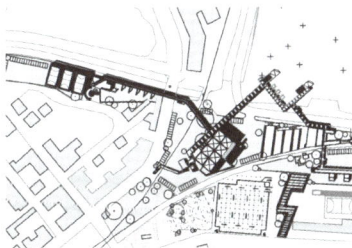

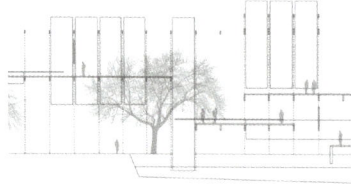

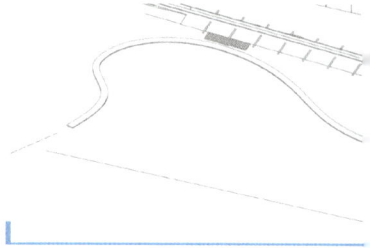

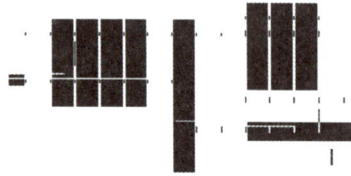

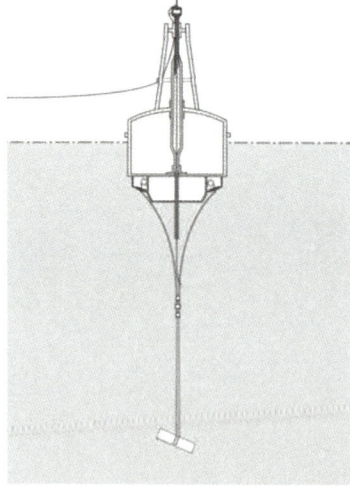

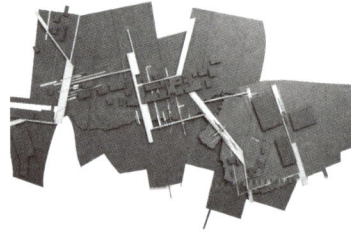

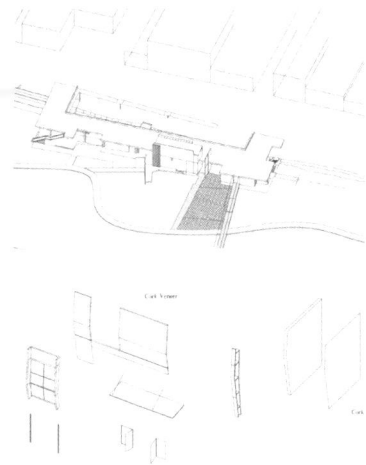

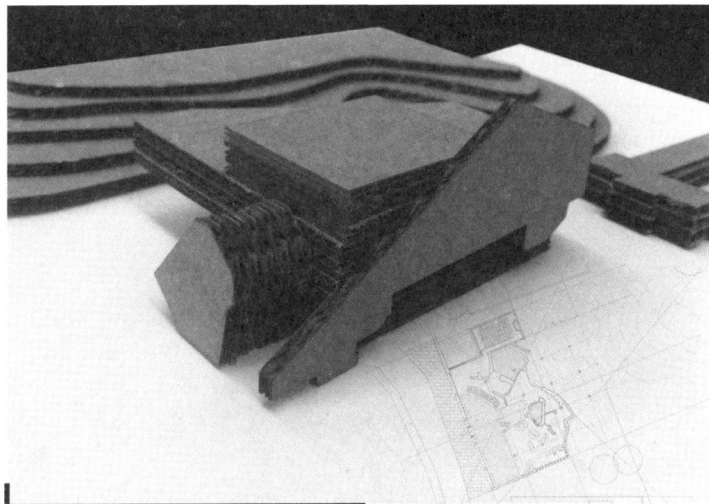

LOVELY BONES

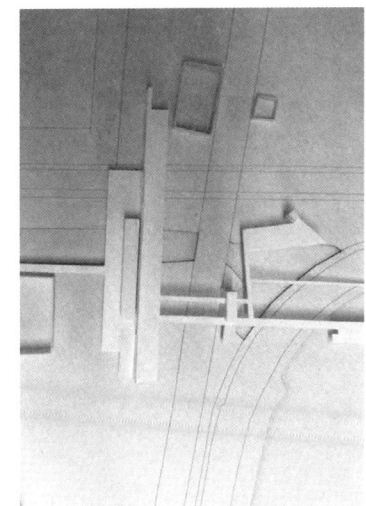

(Amy) Li Bingxin

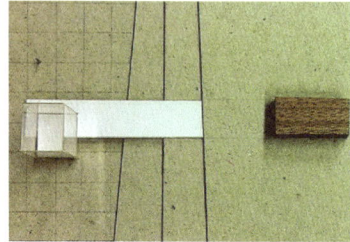

REEDS AND RITUALS

Ritual and
Dwelling
Bio-Fuel
Housing
Civic Halls

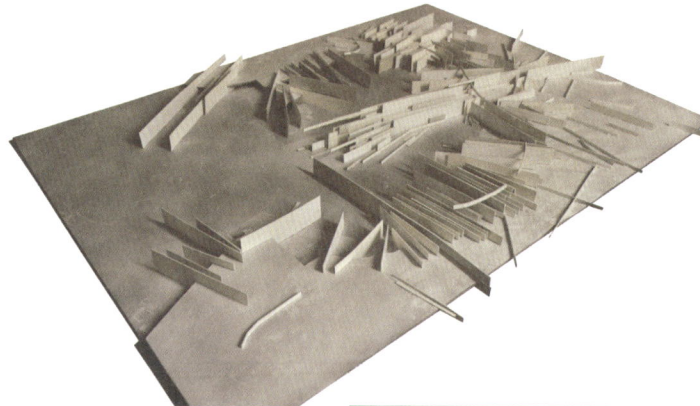

Melinda Jin
(Jack) Weifeng Kong
(Sharon) Shiyun Shen

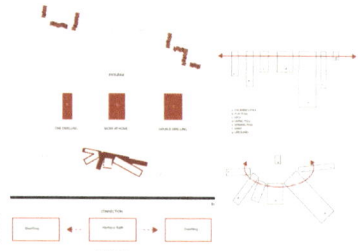

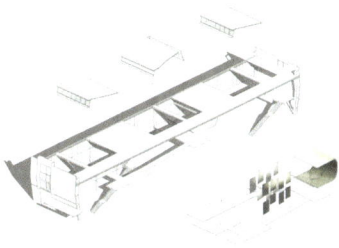

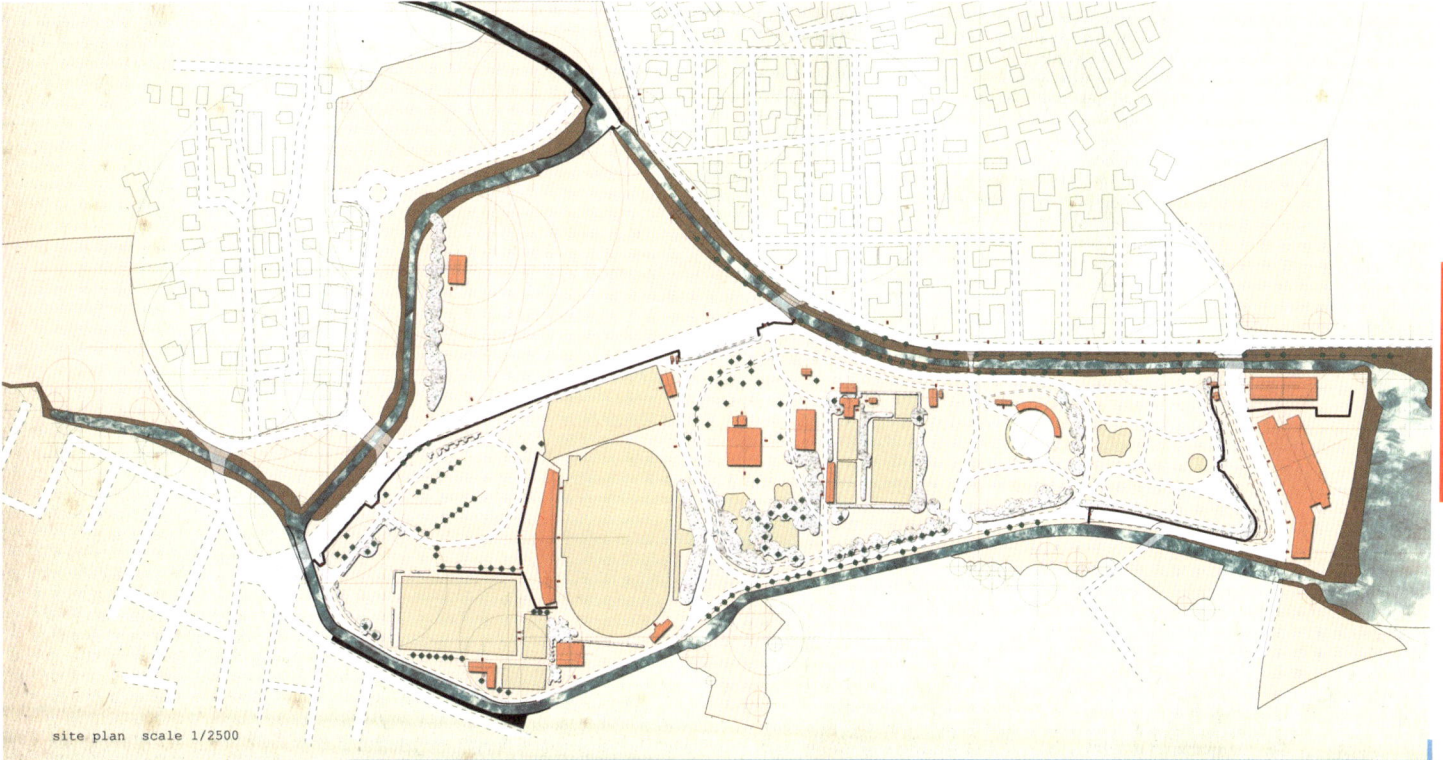

site plan scale 1/2500

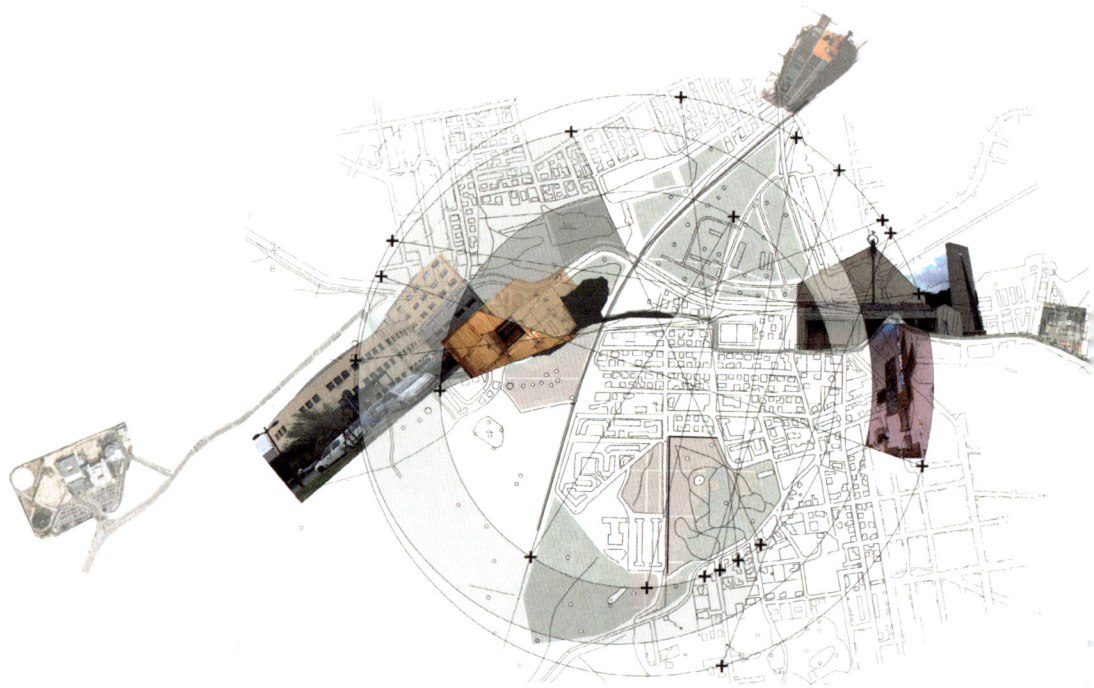

THE PRESENCE OF THE ABSENT

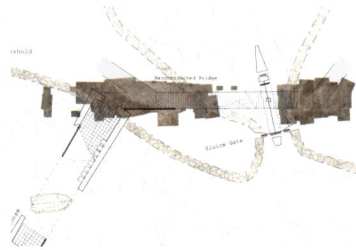

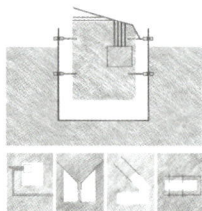

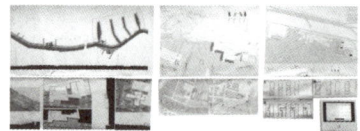

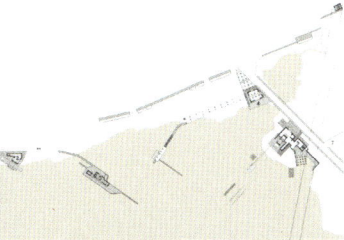

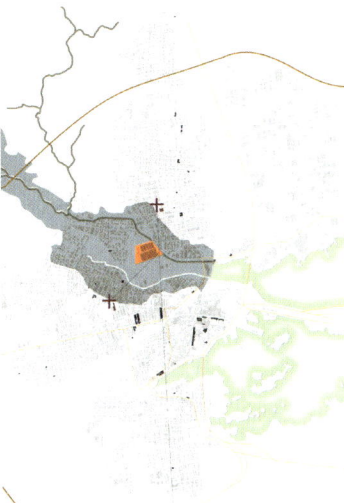

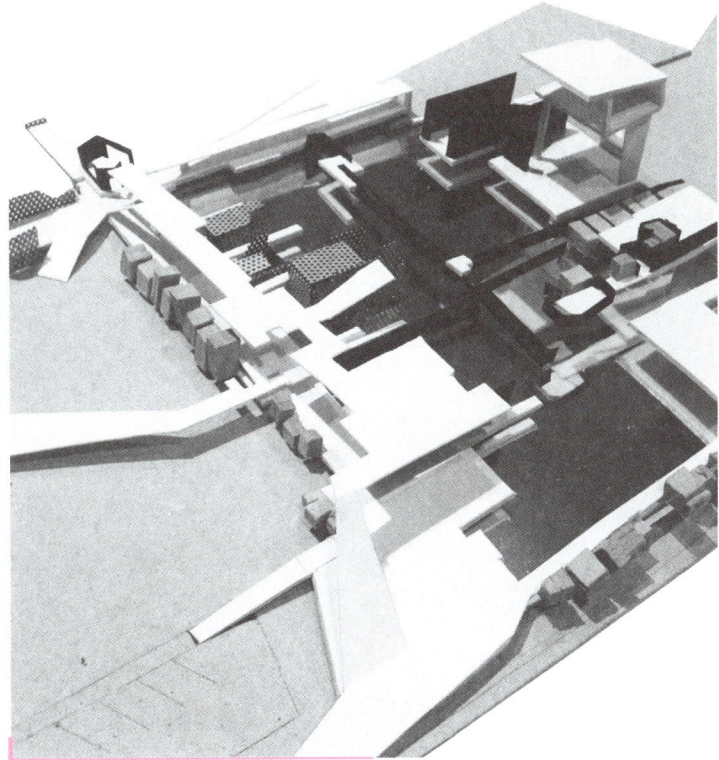

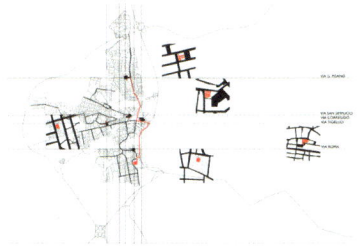

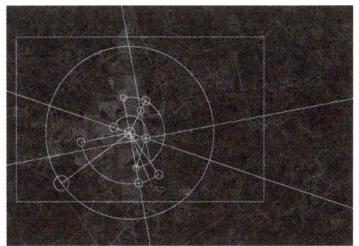

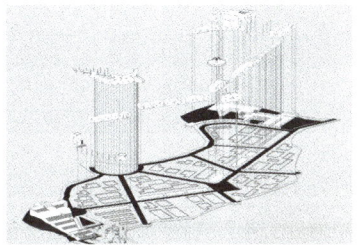

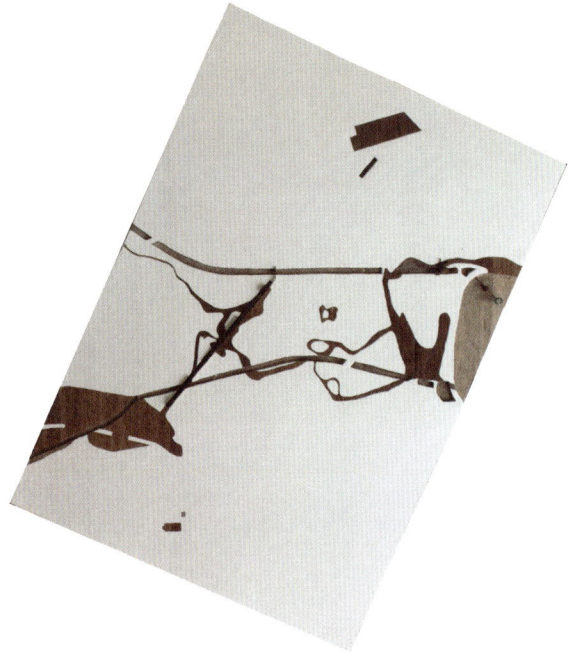

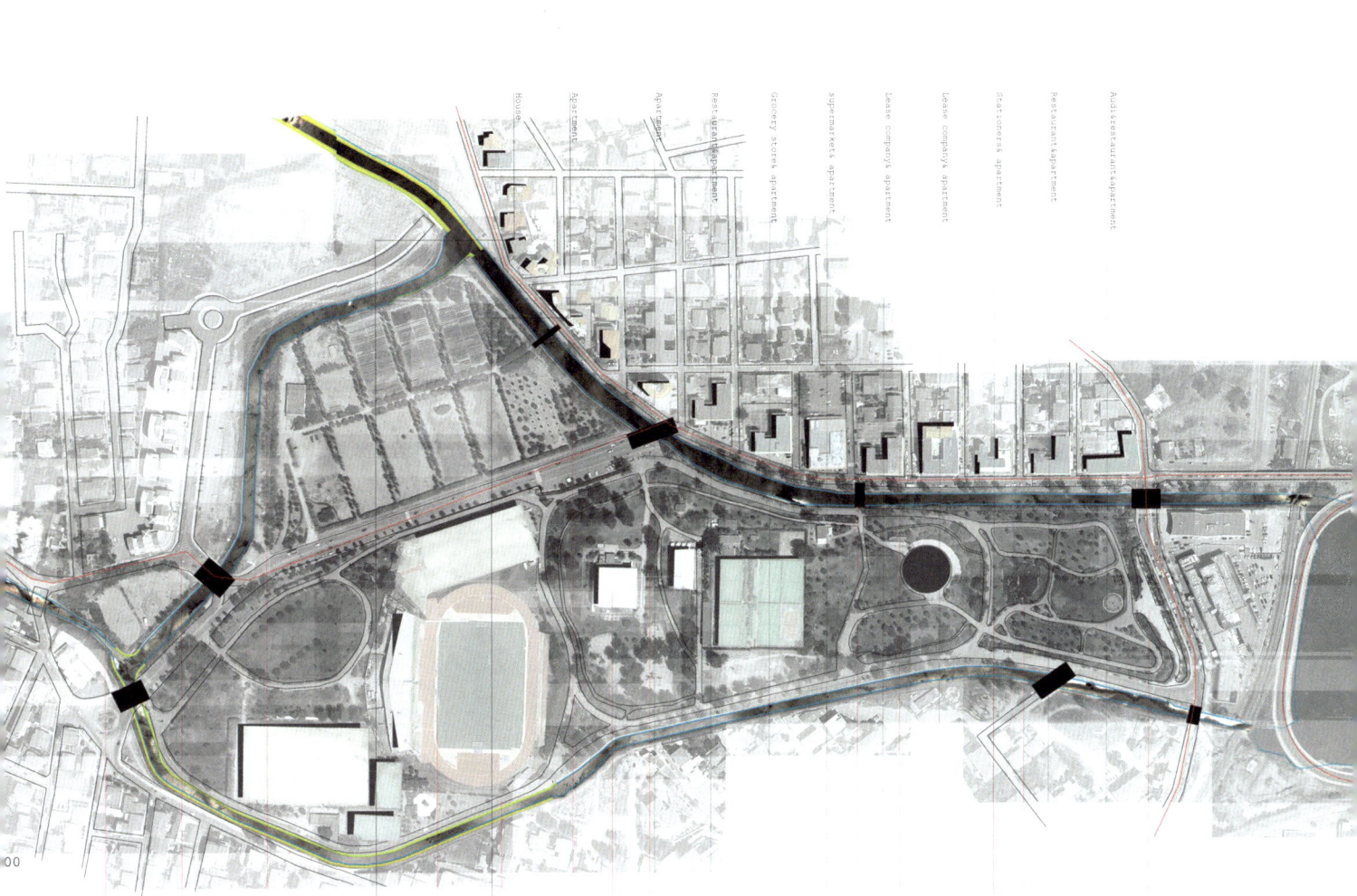

Time & Seasons
Memory
Park and
Facilities

Frame
Technical College

Exchange
Cast
Hauntology
Hand-Craft Market

(Sherry) Liu Yi

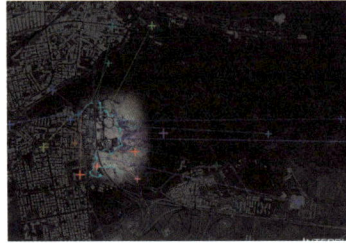

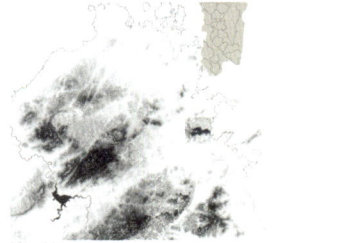

Greenland of Office

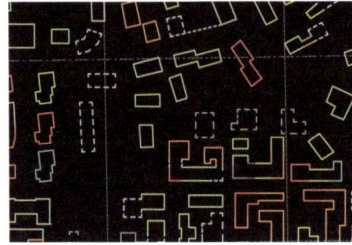

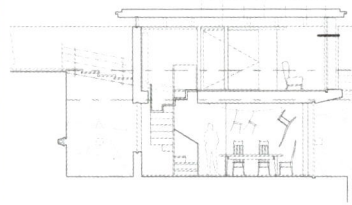

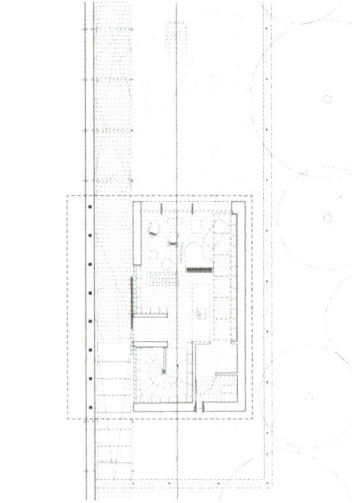

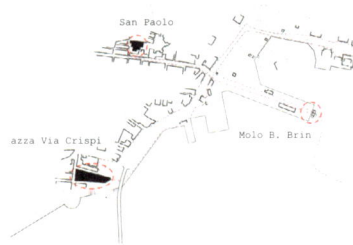

San Paolo

azza Via Crispi

Molo B. Brin

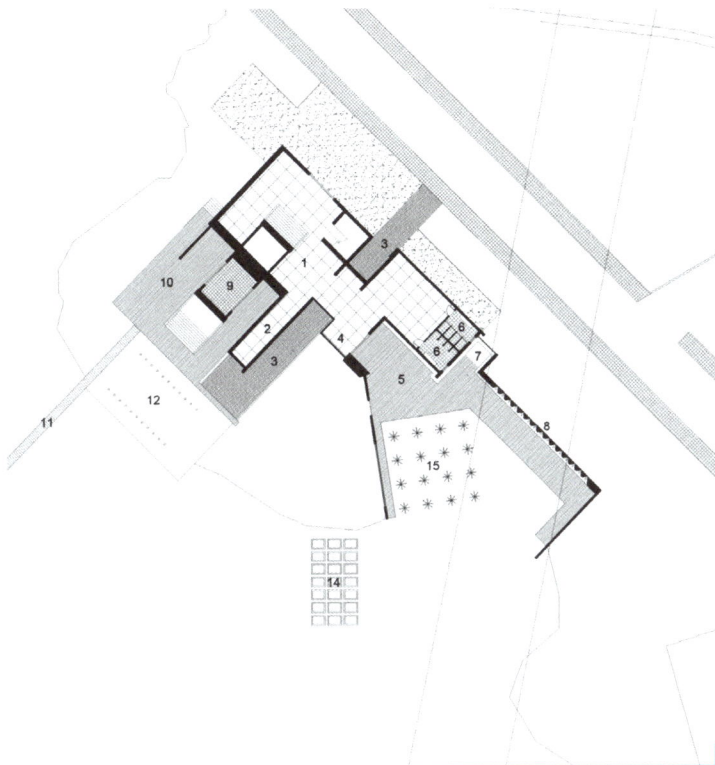

FRAMING

Jørgen Ekerhovd

CLAY HAUNTOLOGY

(Katie) Qing Shao

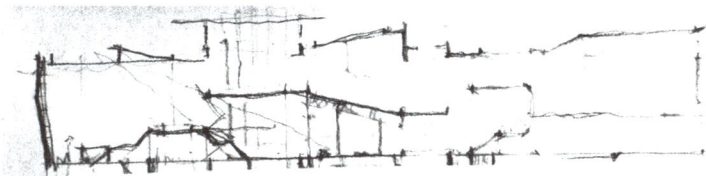

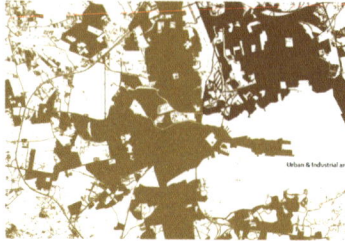

Pink Blush
Pickleweed
Products

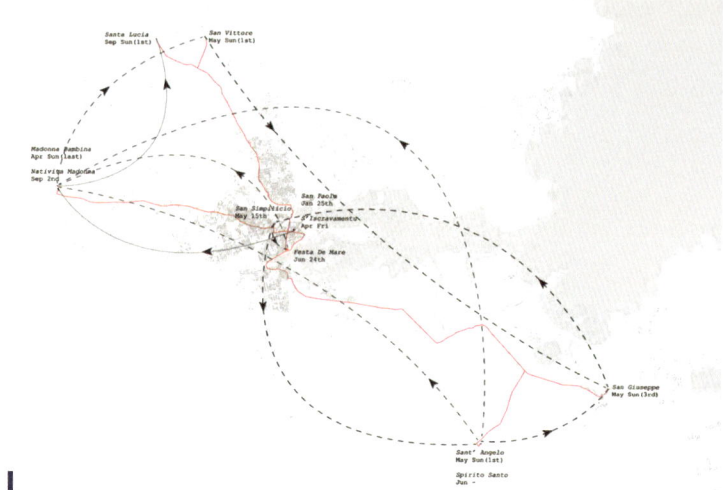

TICKLED PICKLEWEED PINK

Jennifer Robertson

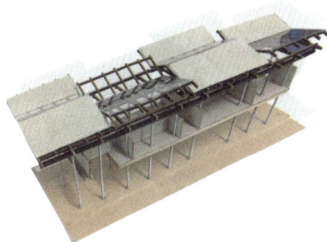
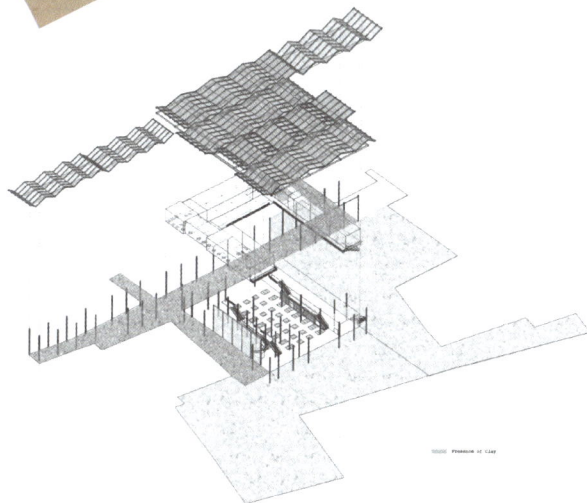

TITLE Presence of Clay

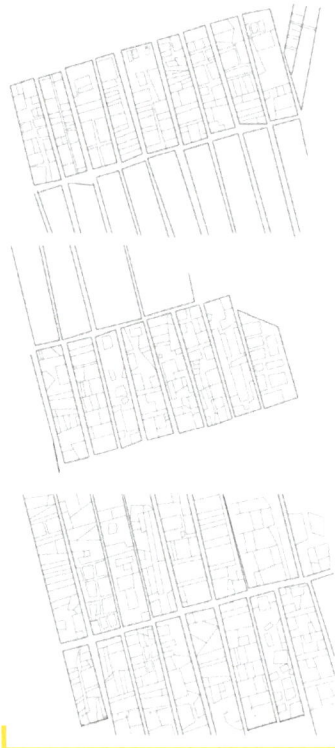

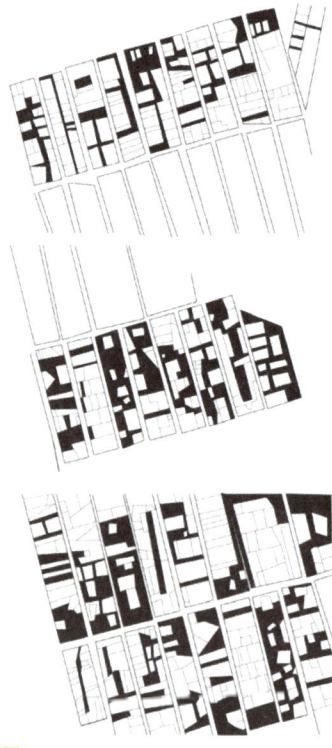

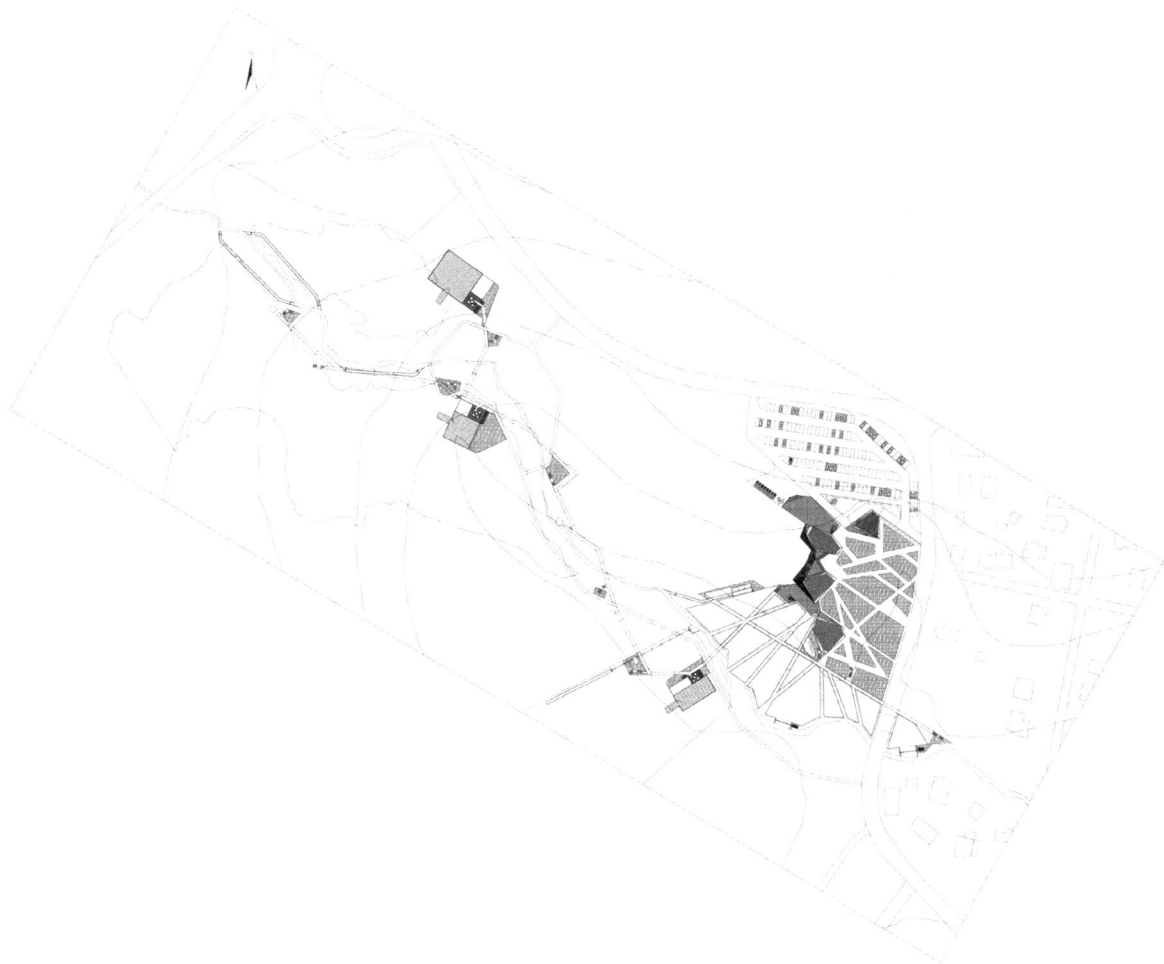

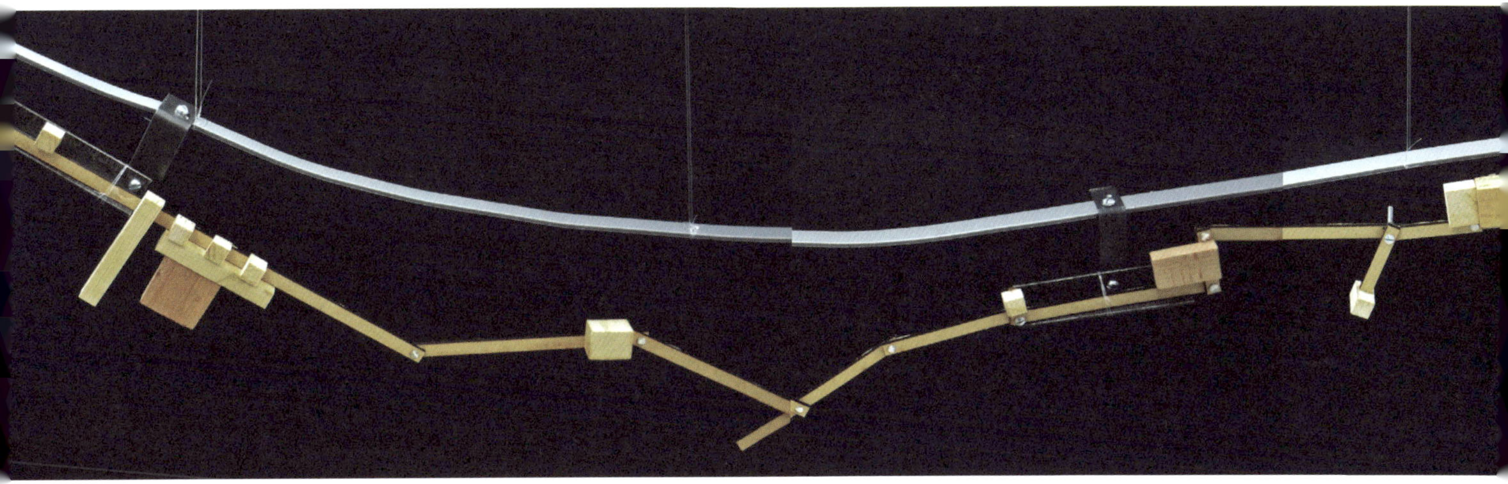

c04_Agora

c03_Education

c02_Artefacts of the city

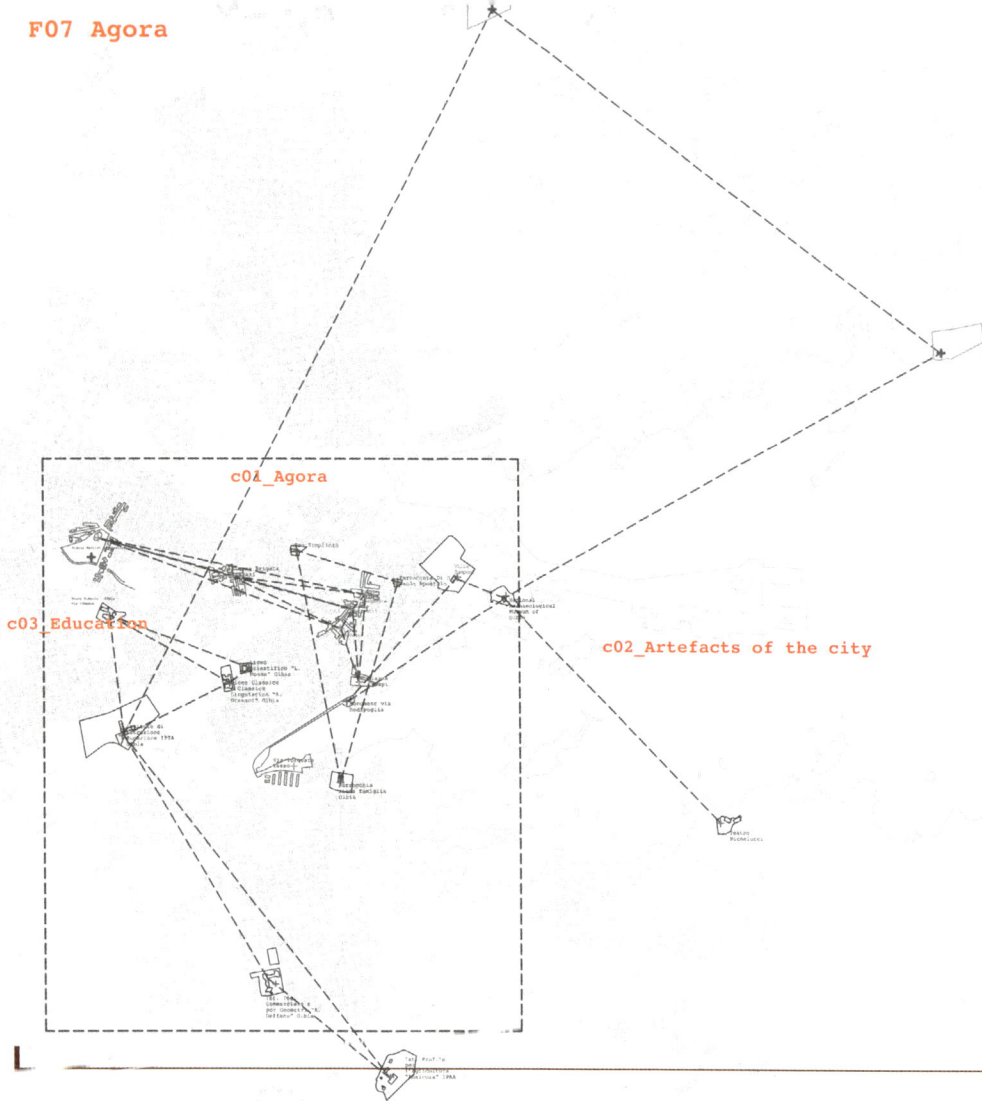

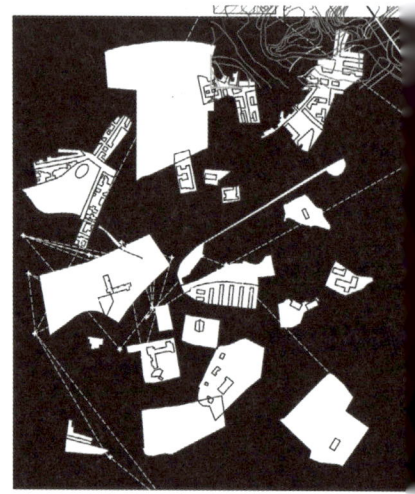

A/C02_Olbia as Archipelago

Scaling to frame

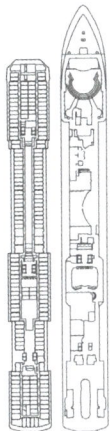

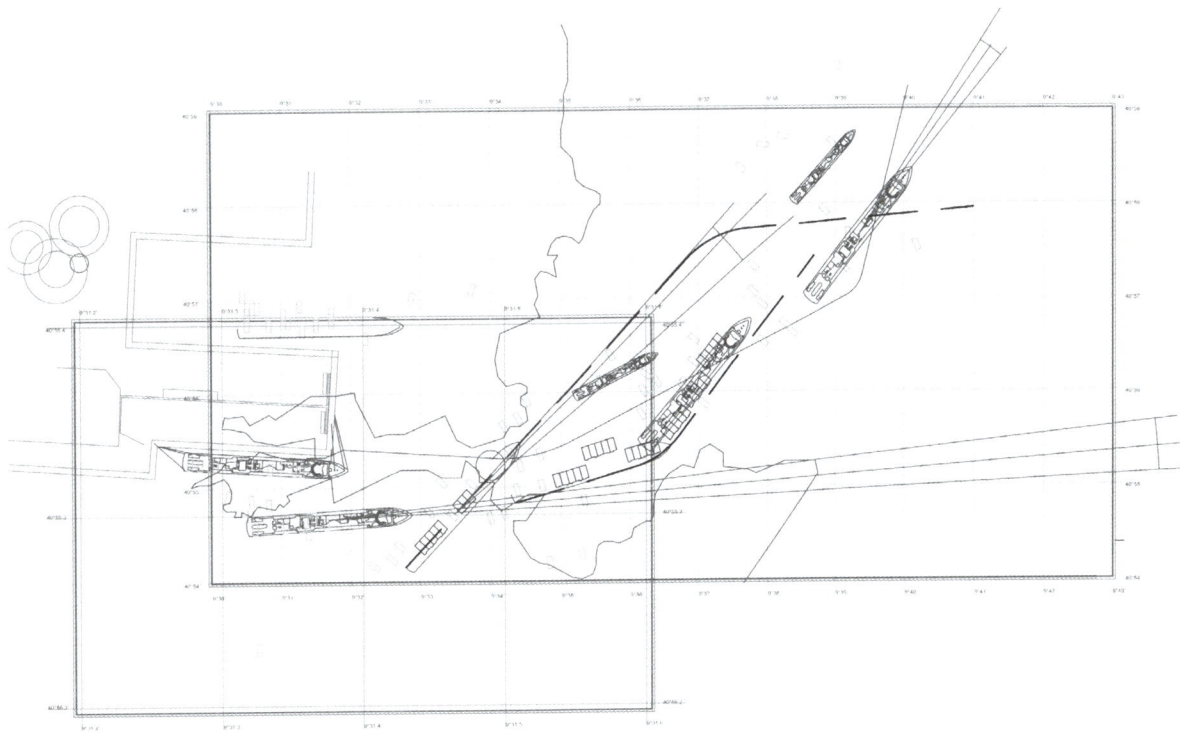

A02_Navigation

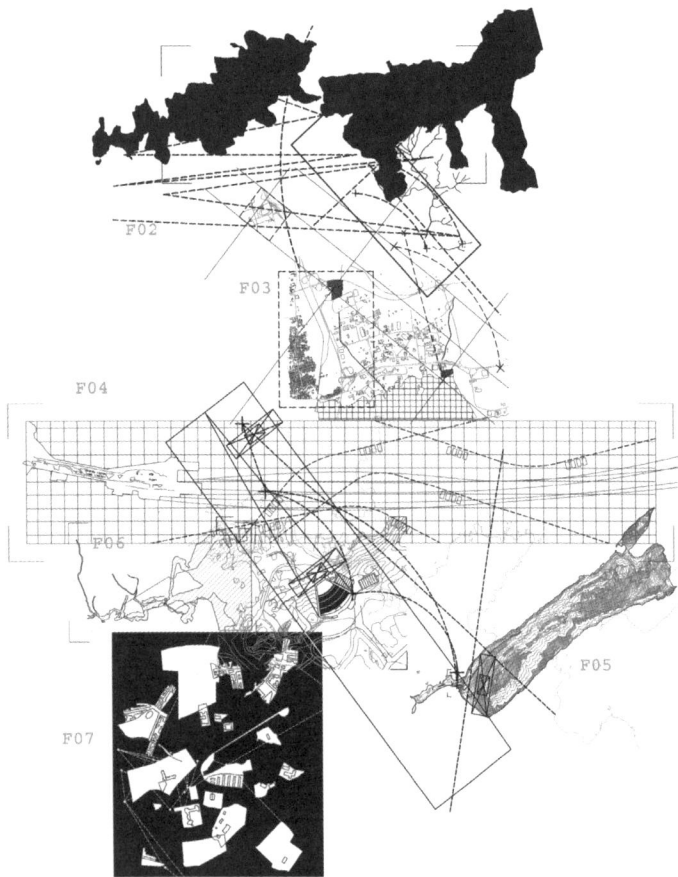

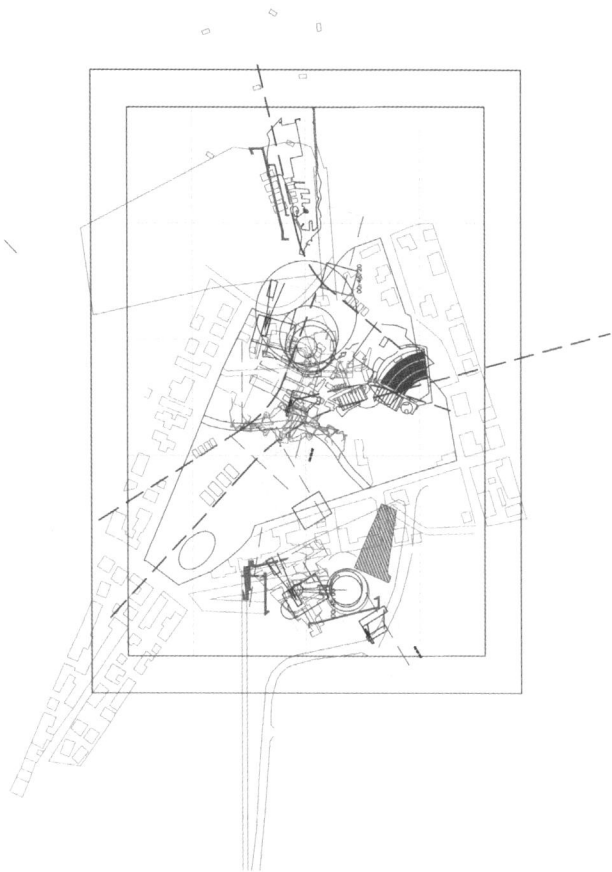

F02

F03

F04

F05

F06

F07

F05

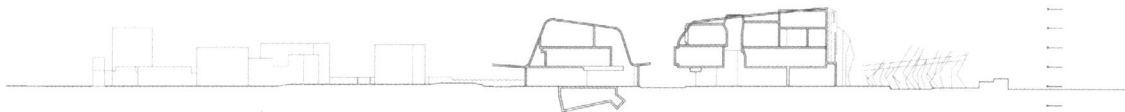

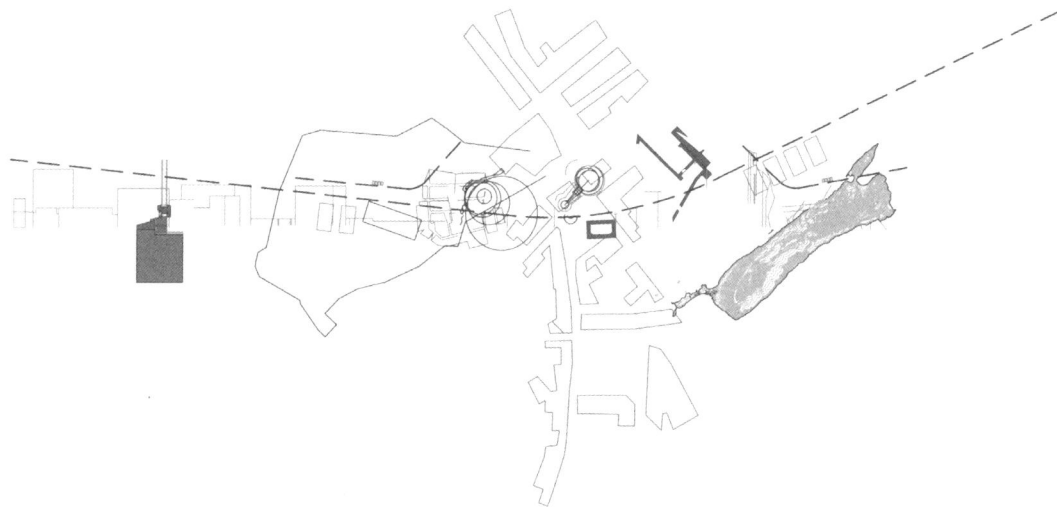

Evocation
Invocation
Theatres

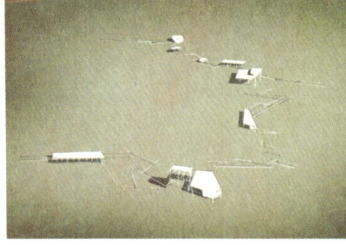

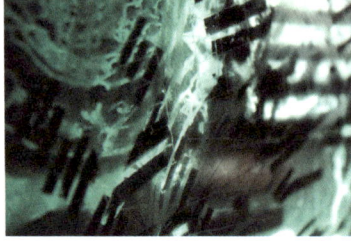

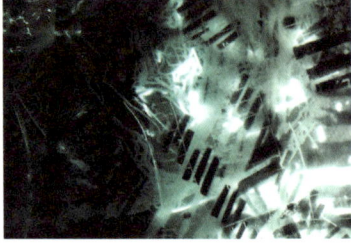

Legacy
Dwelling
Hauntology
Hall
Housing
Museum
Silt
Industries

SOUTH BAY PERFORMATIVITY

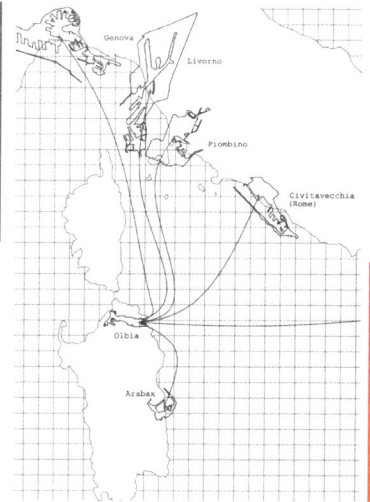

(Eric) Wen Yucong

GRANITE, LIGHT AND
CATCHING SILT

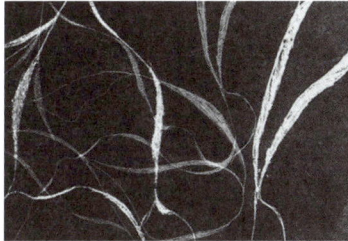

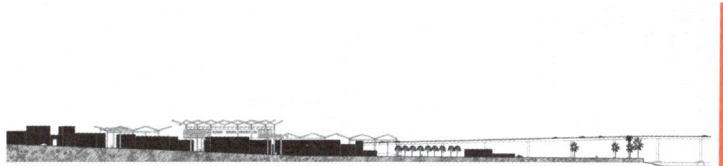

(Ethan) Huining Li
(Wayne) Jinwu Wei

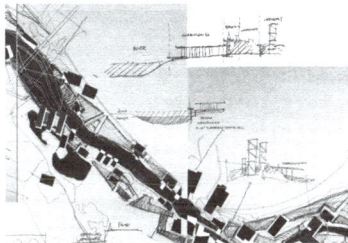

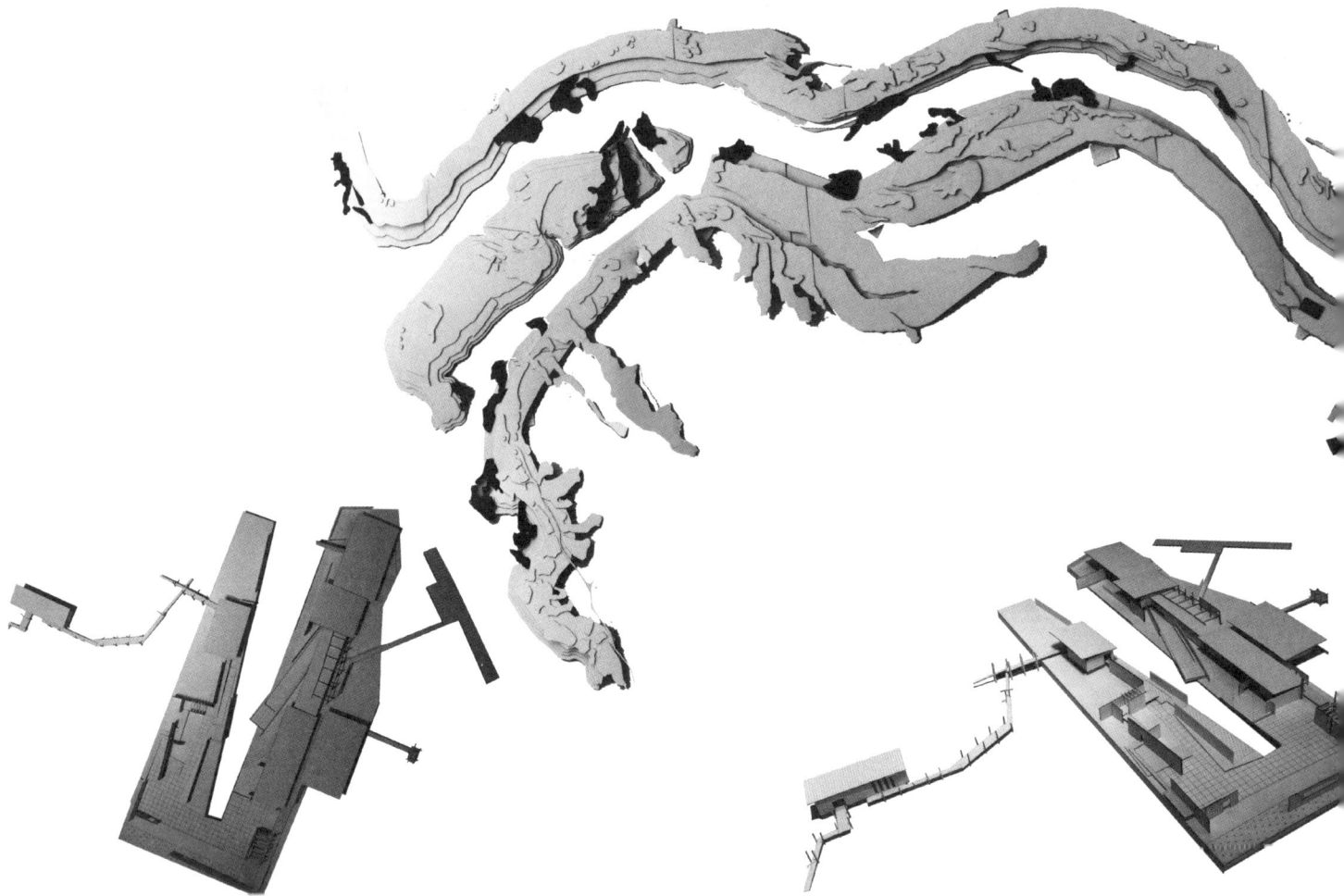

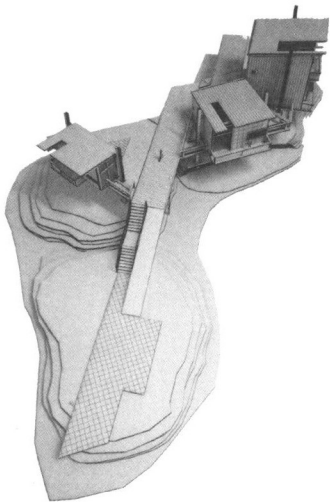

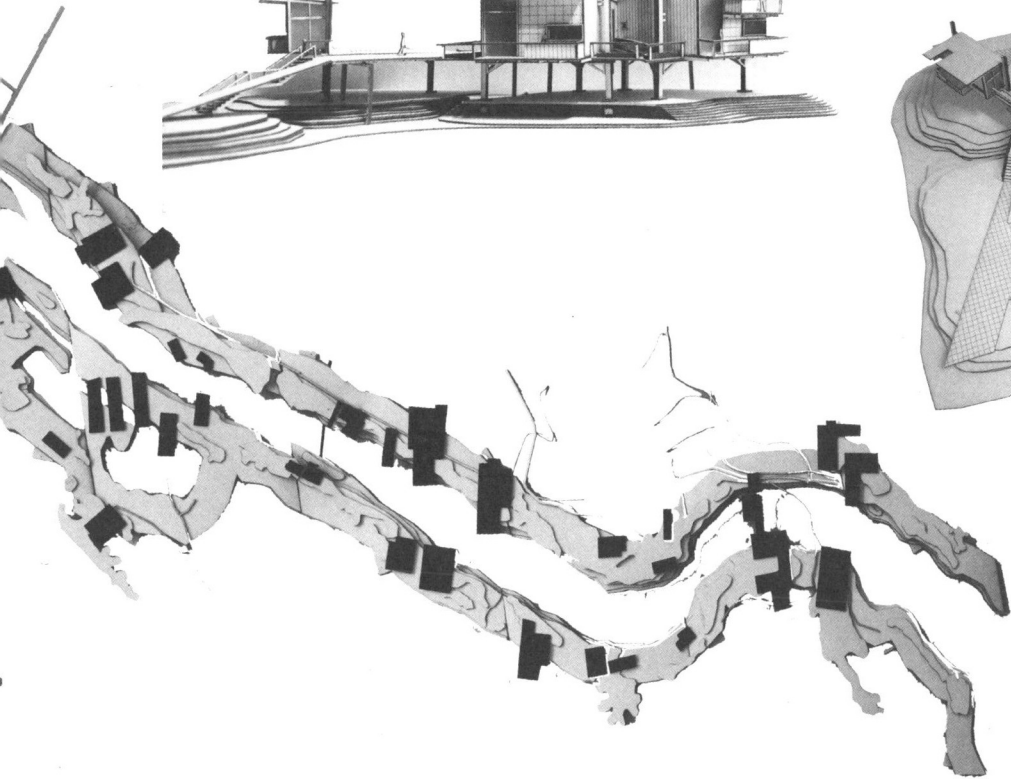

CORK BARK AND GRANITE BITE

Neil Cunning

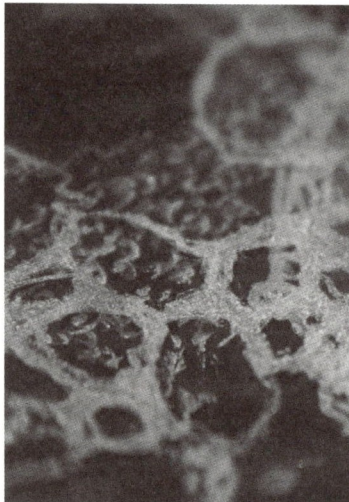

VOIDS IN THE CITY

(Wendy) Sixiao Zhan

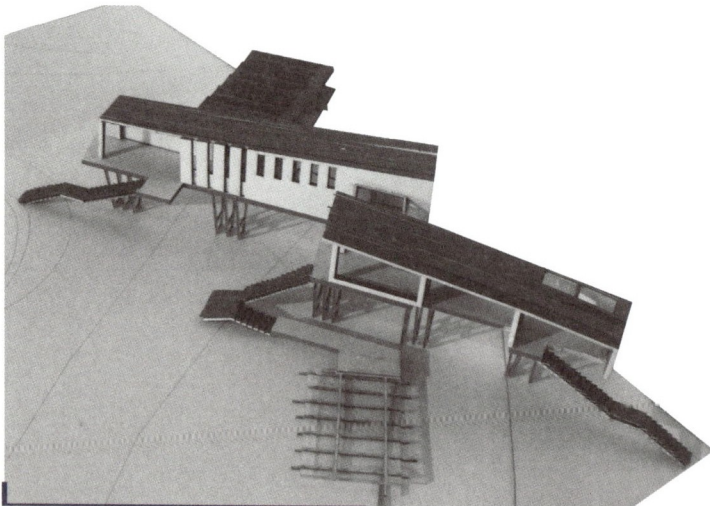

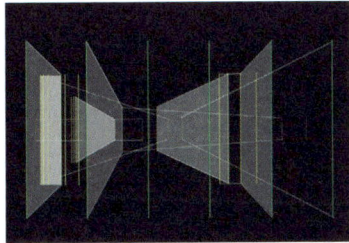
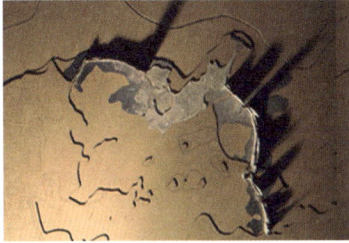

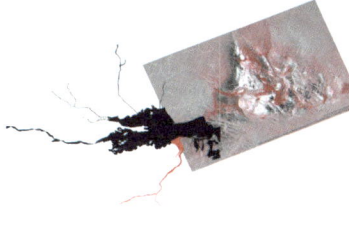

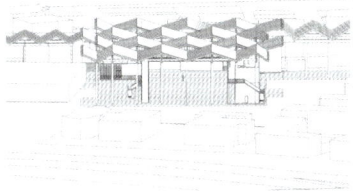

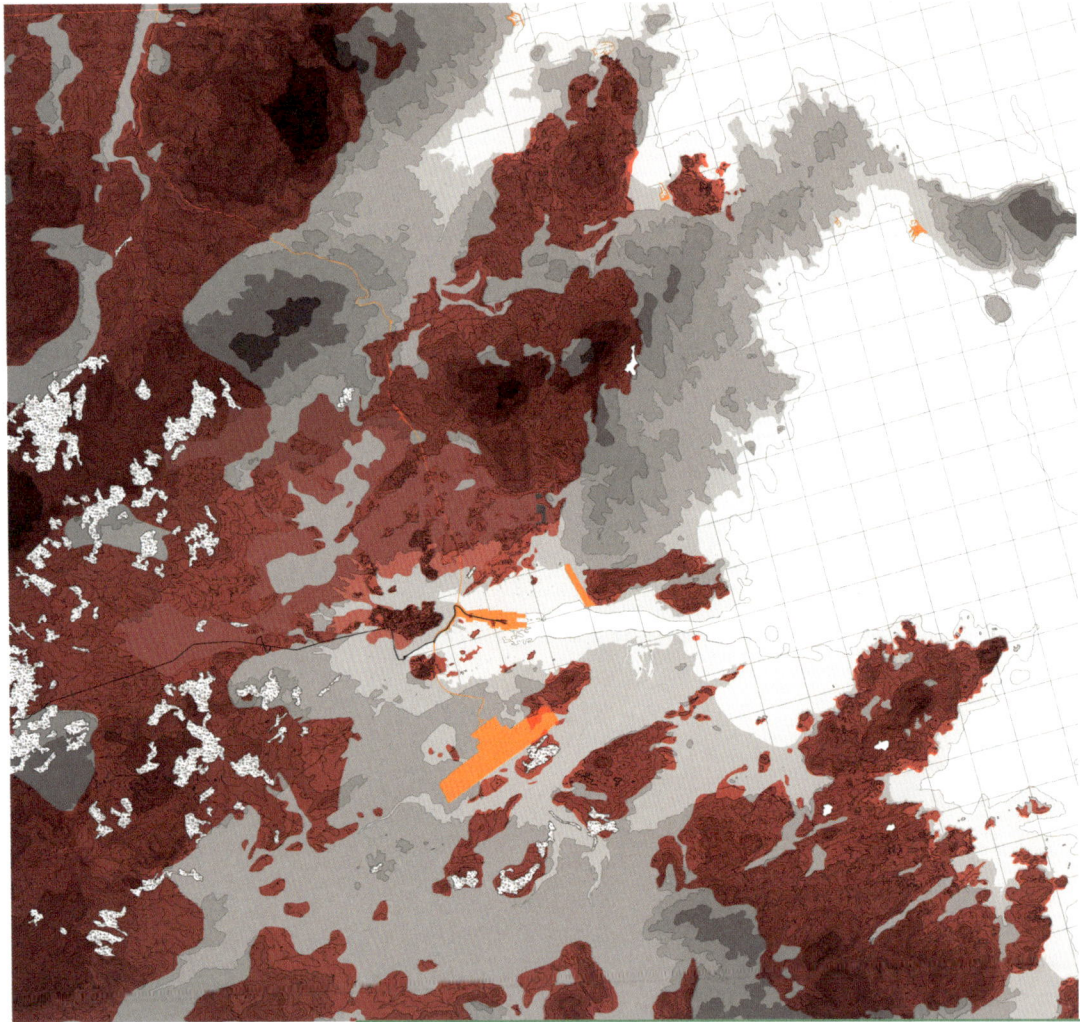

Agencies on Isola Bianca

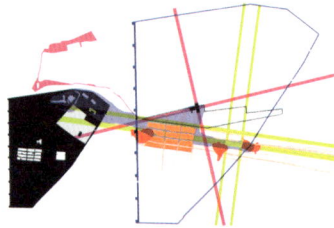

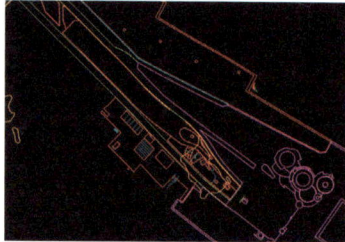

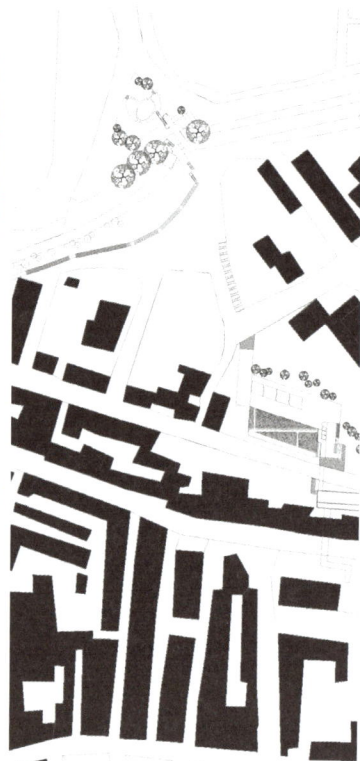

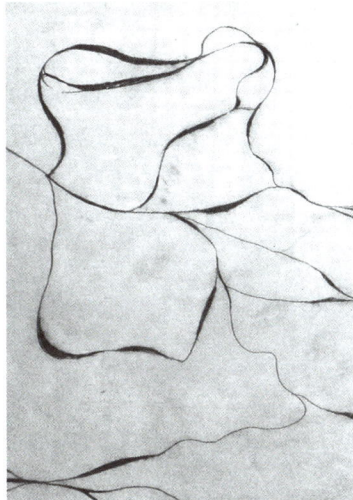

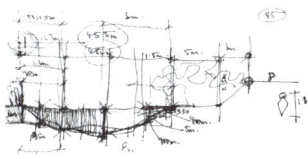

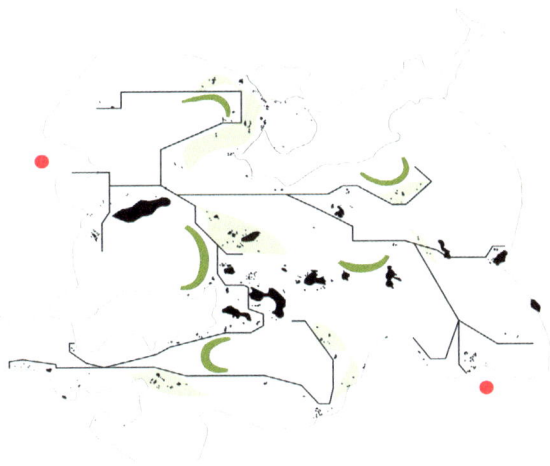

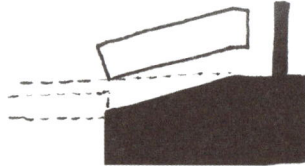

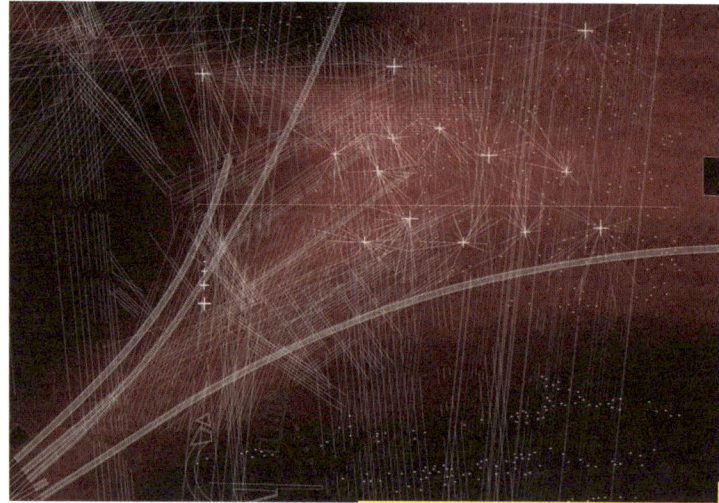

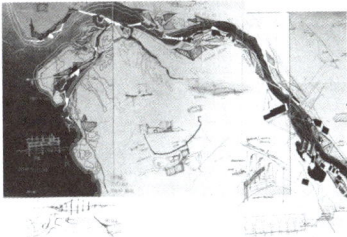
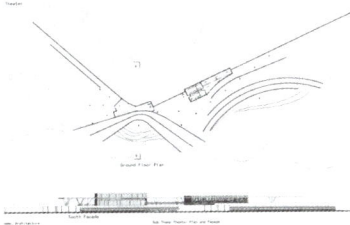
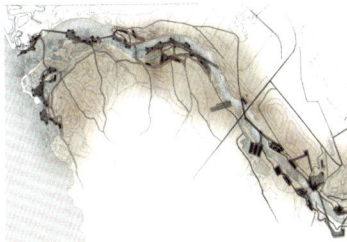

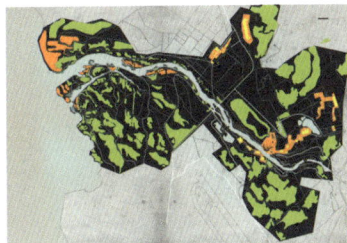
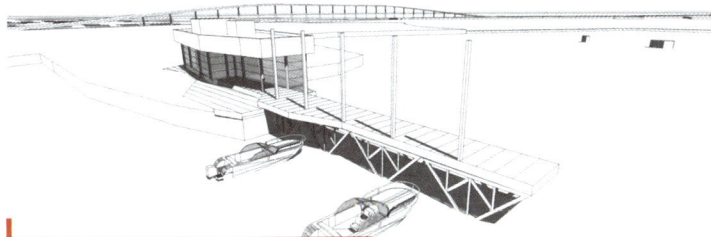

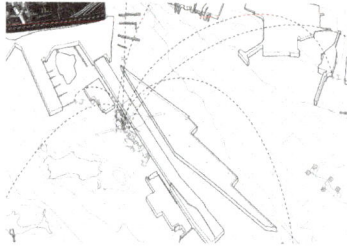

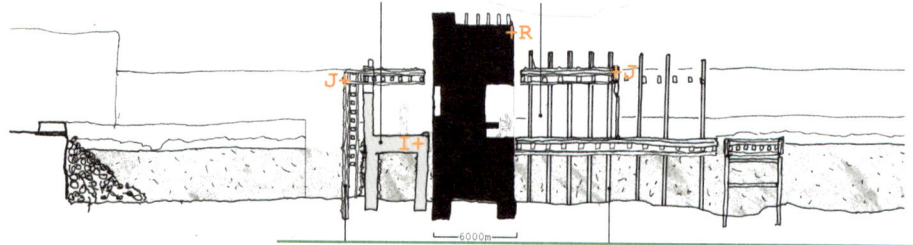

J+ +R +J

I+

6000m

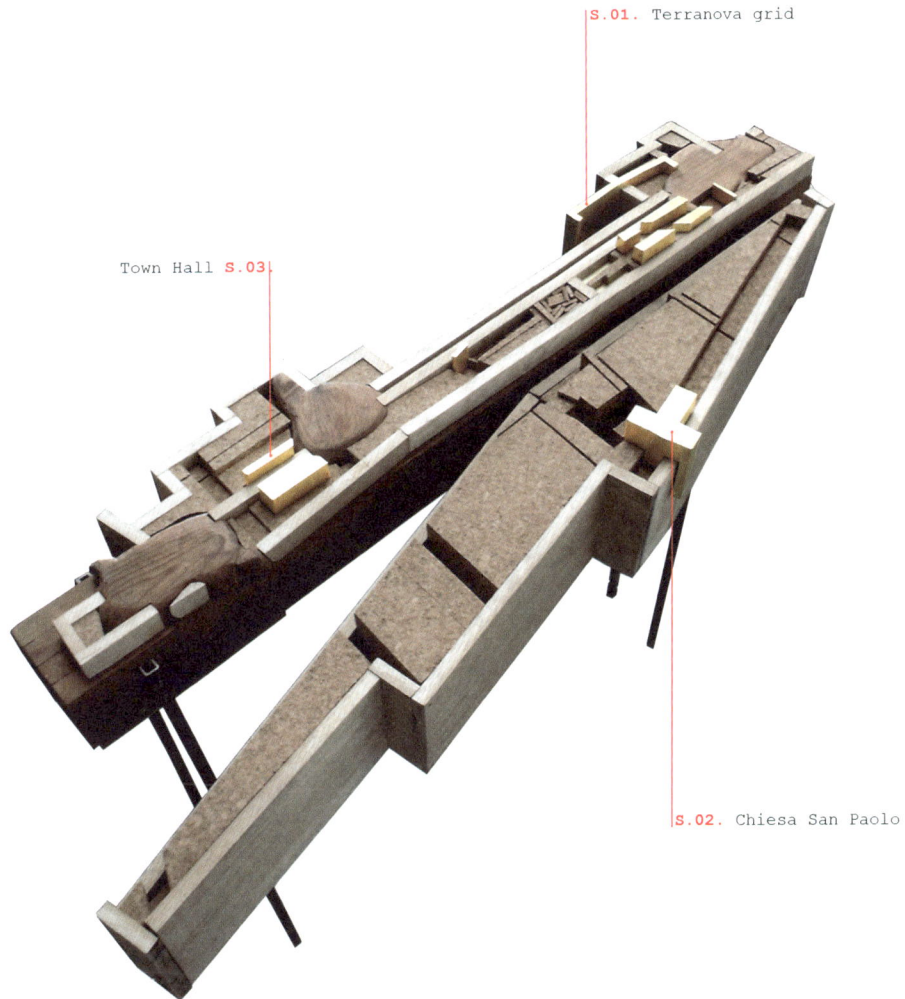

S.01. Terranova grid

Town Hall S.03.

S.02. Chiesa San Paolo

Palimpsest
Life-Story
Live-Project

Boat
Builders
Scrapyard
Rowing Club

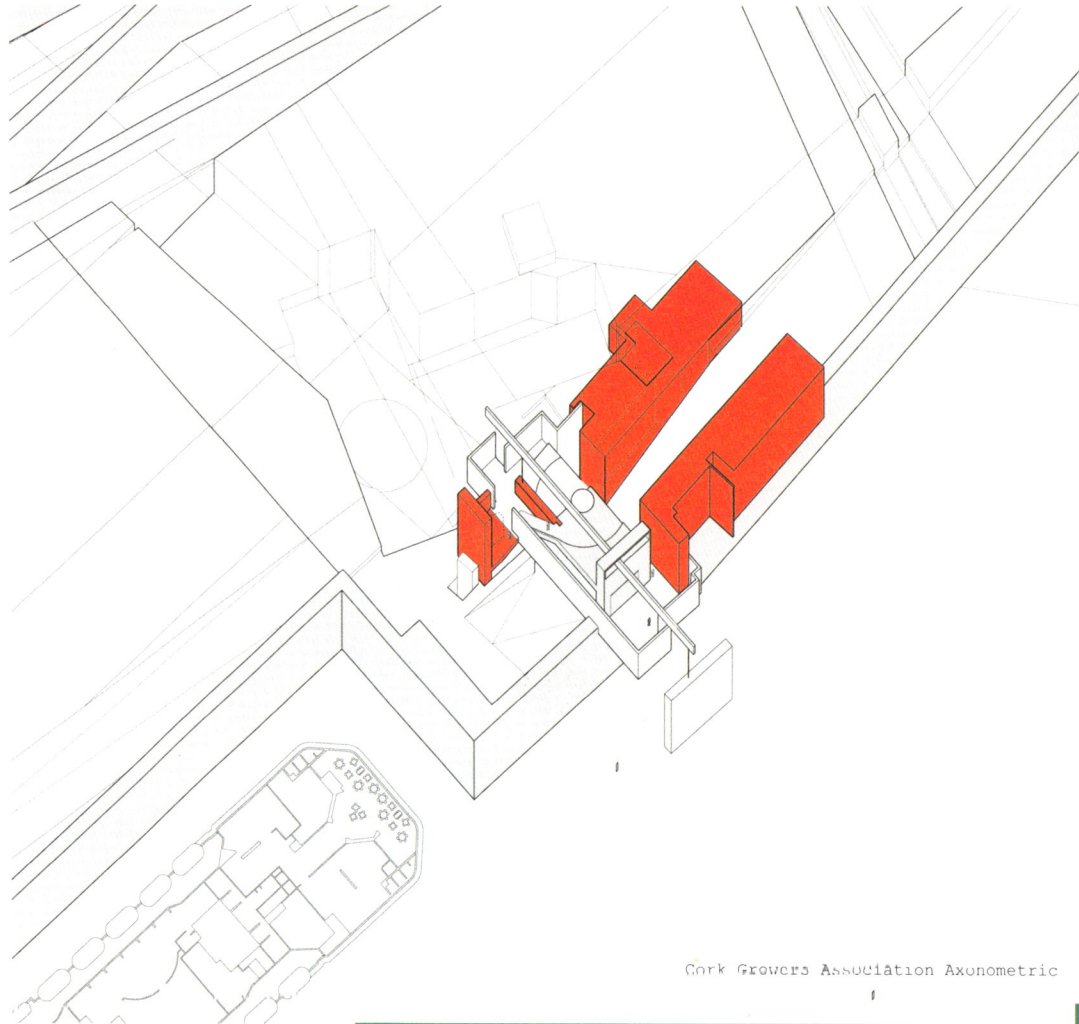

Cork Growers Association Axonometric

FILO FRAGMENT FICTIONS

Jamie Kinghorn
Louisa Butler

Exchange
Seduction
Suggestion
Stock-
Exchange
Wool
Fish
Bread
Granite

Angel Hsiao

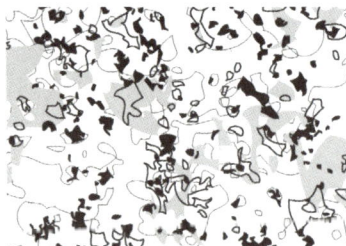

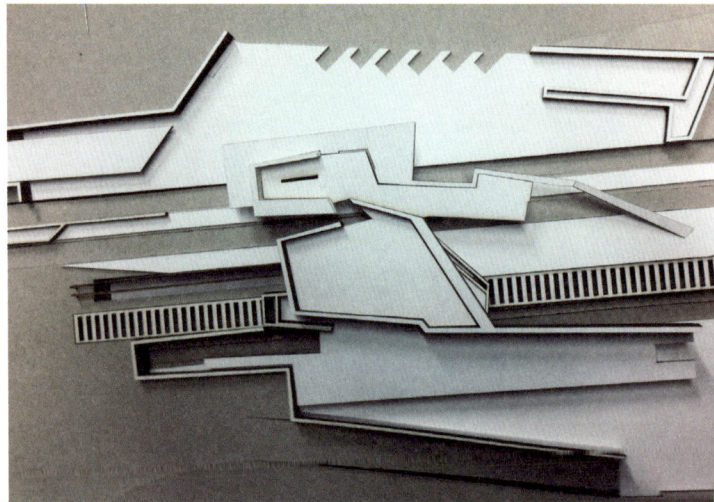

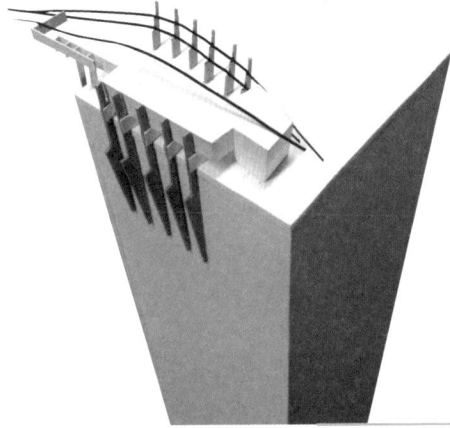

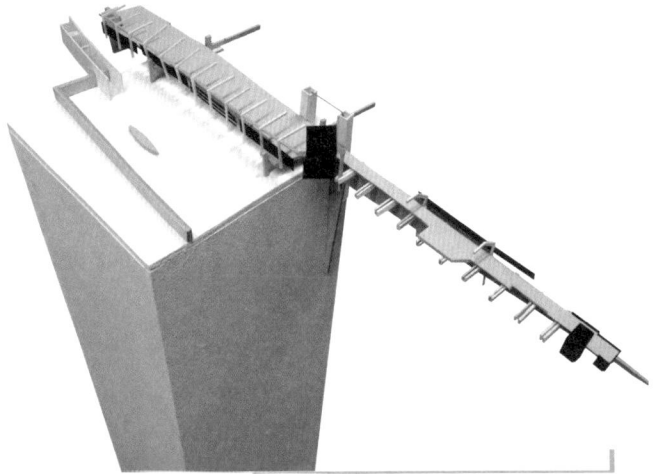

Proportion
Mussel Farm
Restaurant

Non-Conformity
Hauntology
Museum
Market

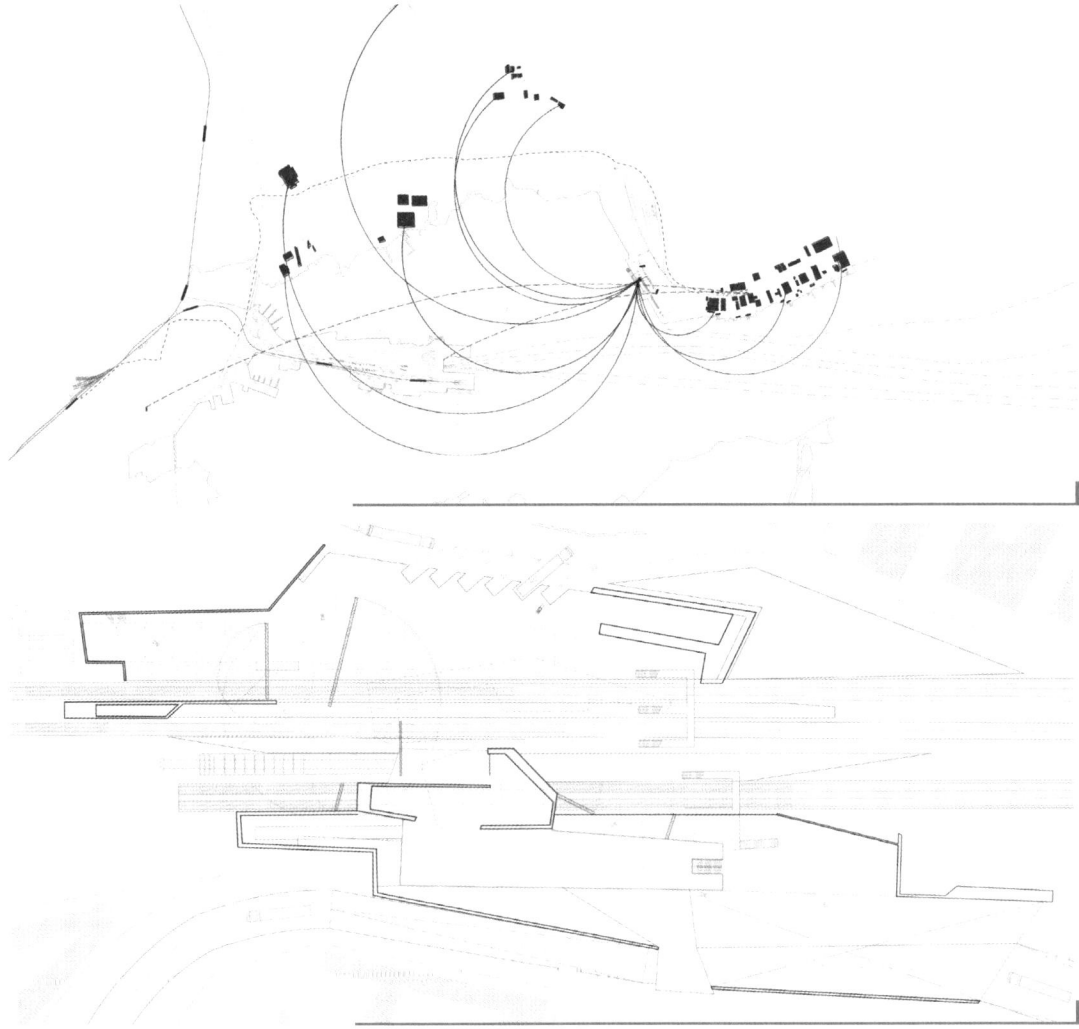

MUSSEL LINES

Oliver Wit

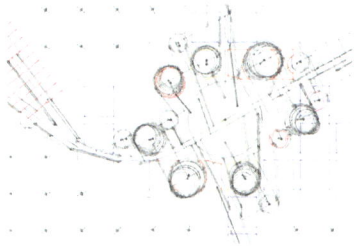

GRAFFITI

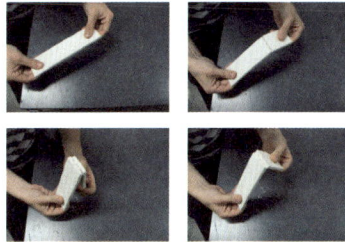

(Simon) Su Junhua

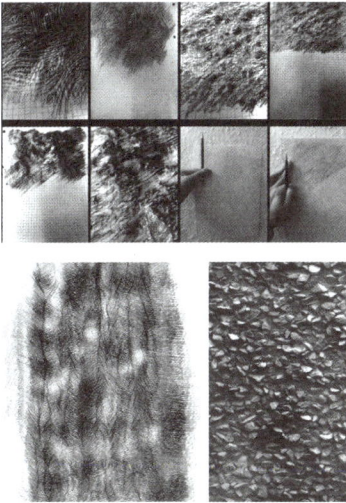

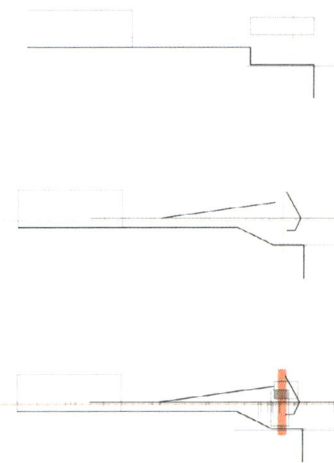

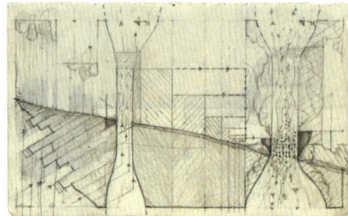

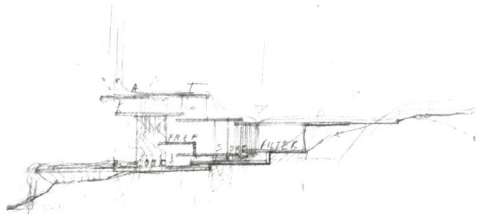

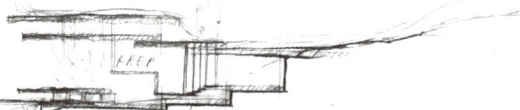

GROWTH

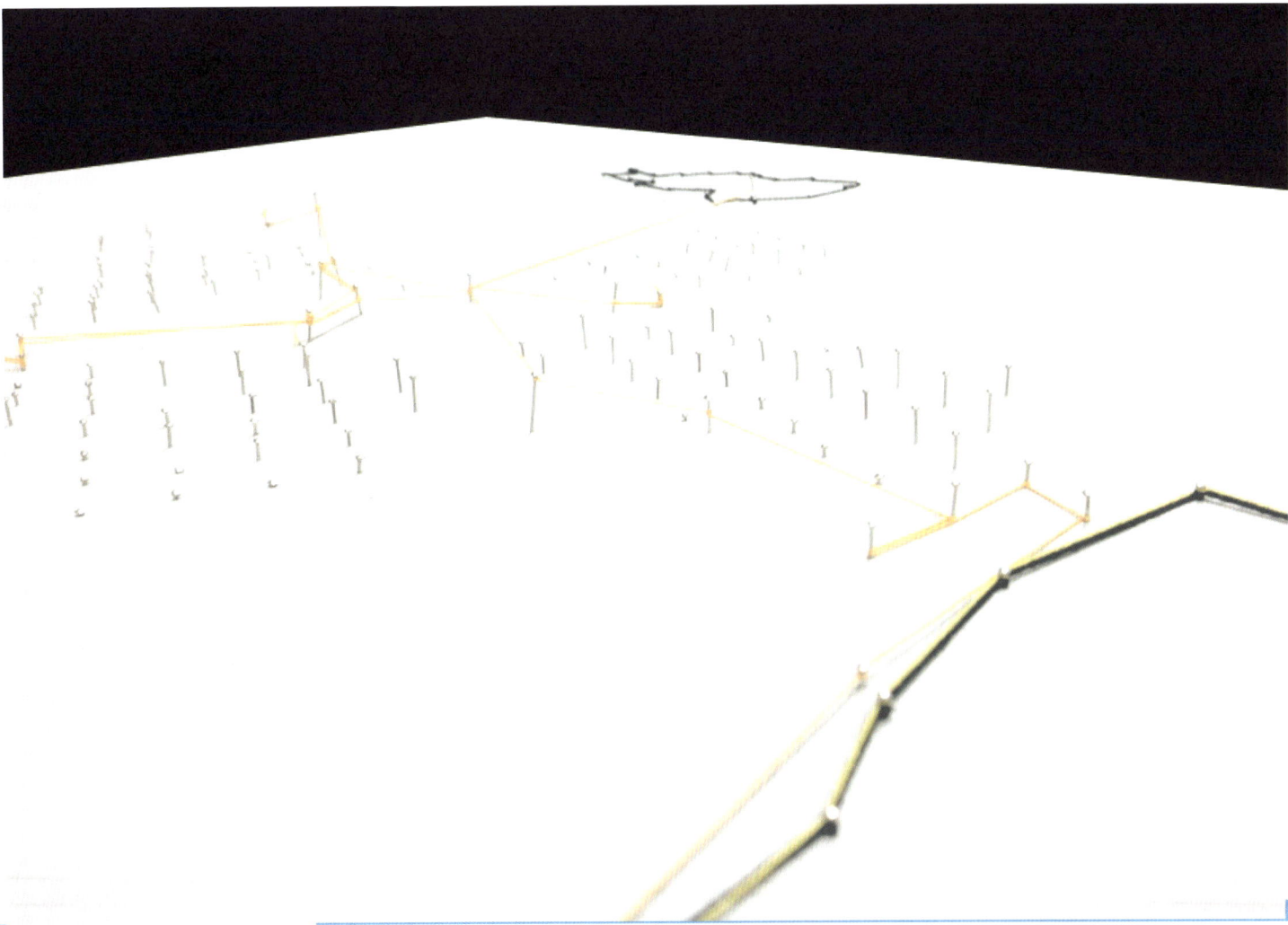

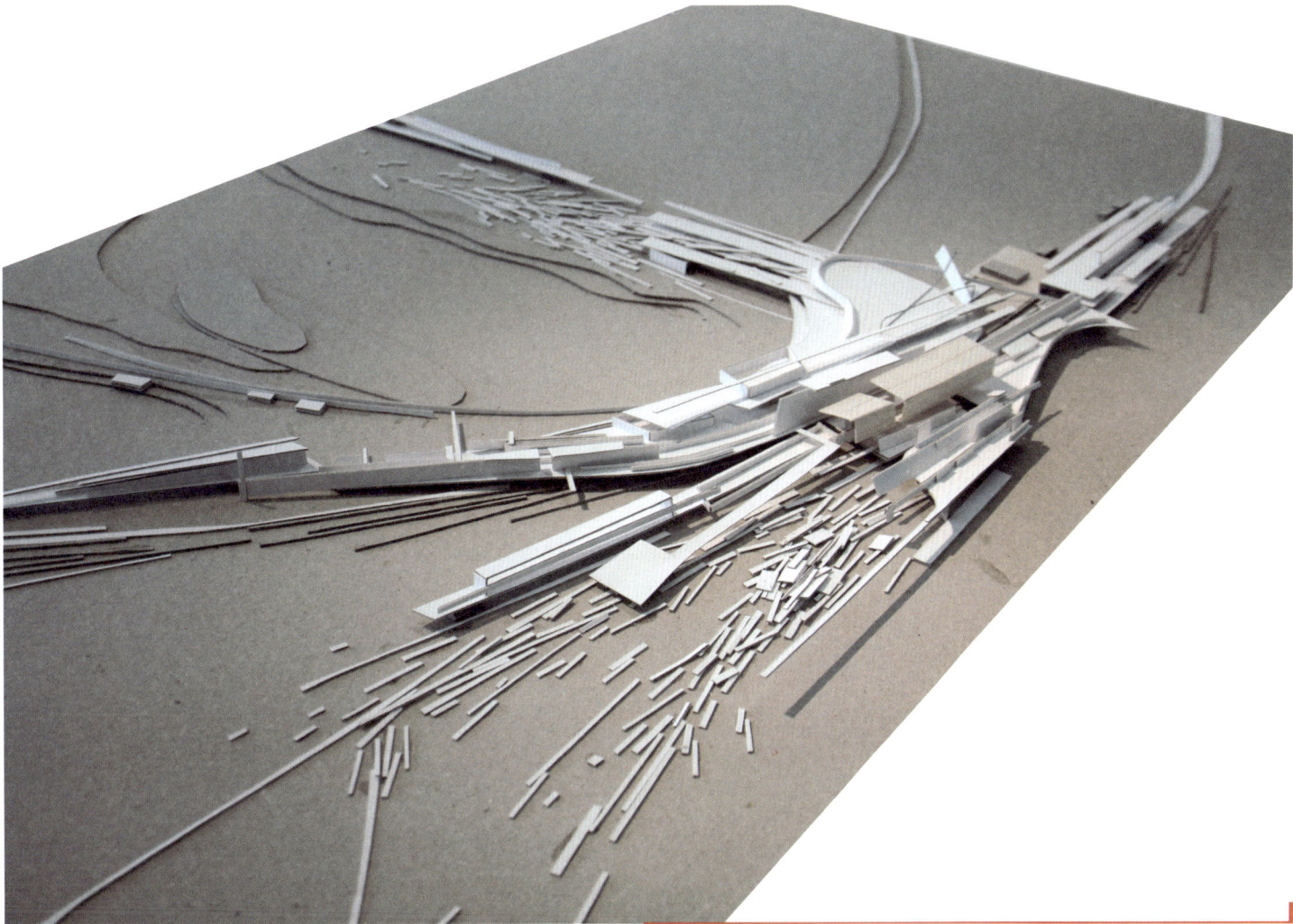

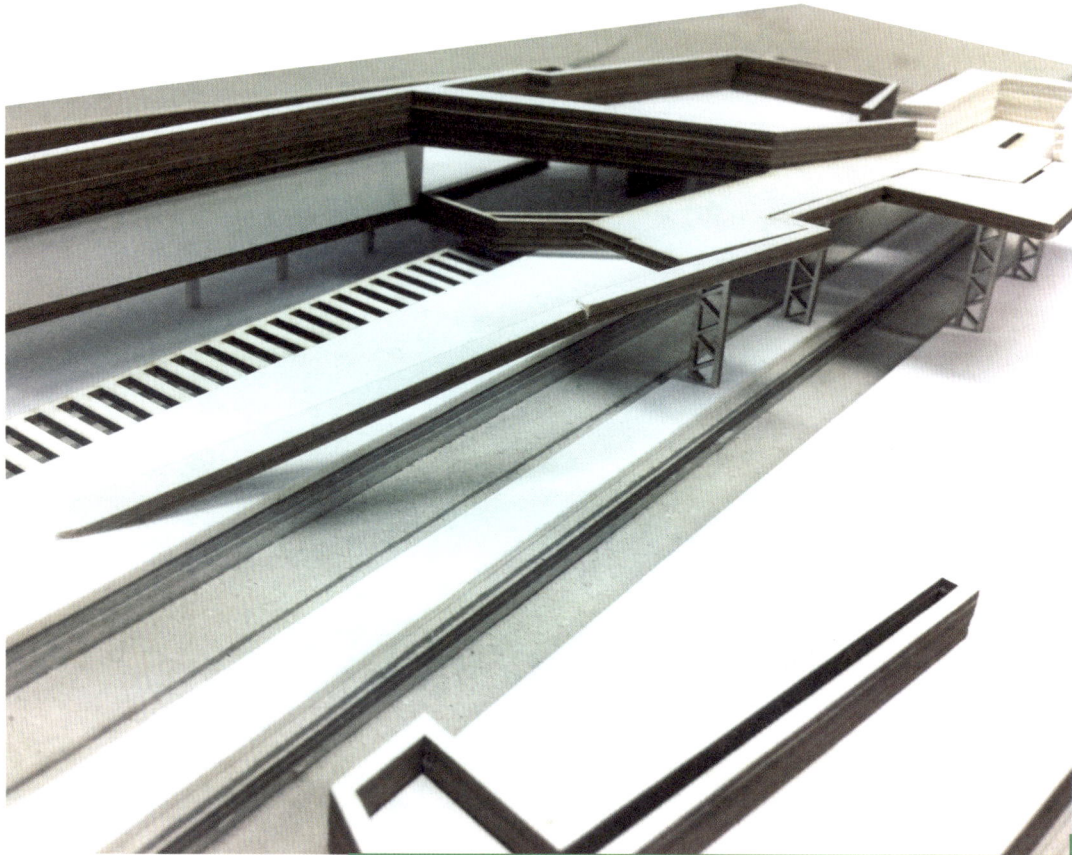

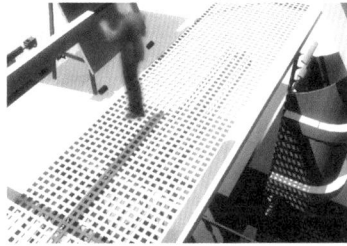

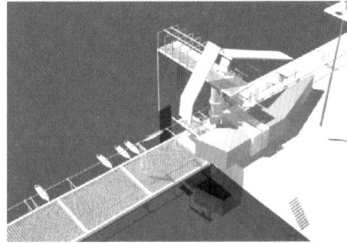

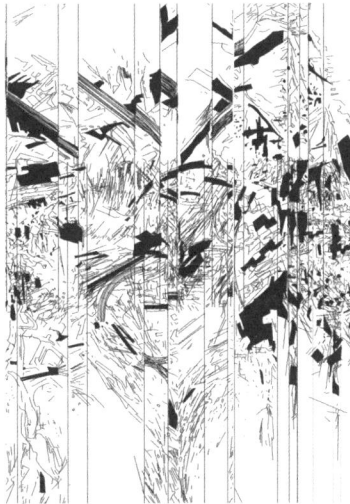

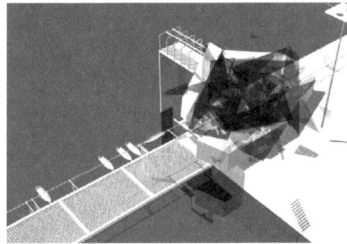

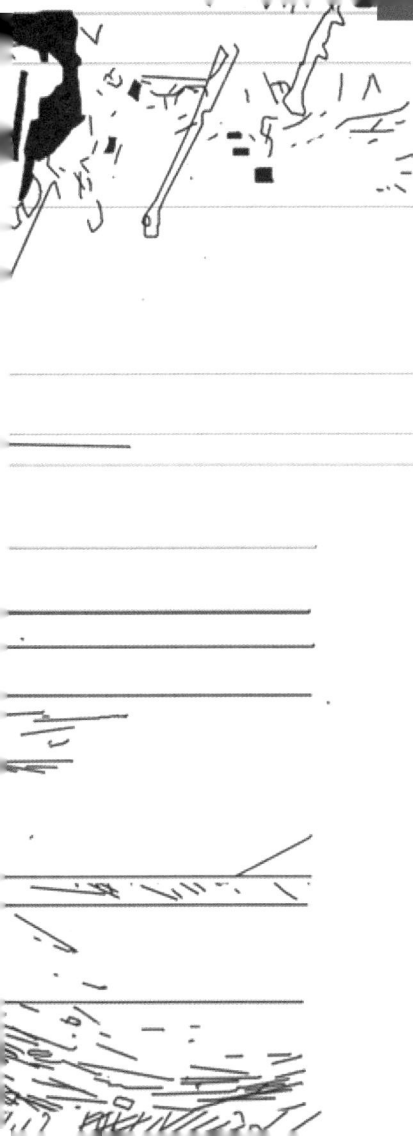

this is the new

map of hauntology

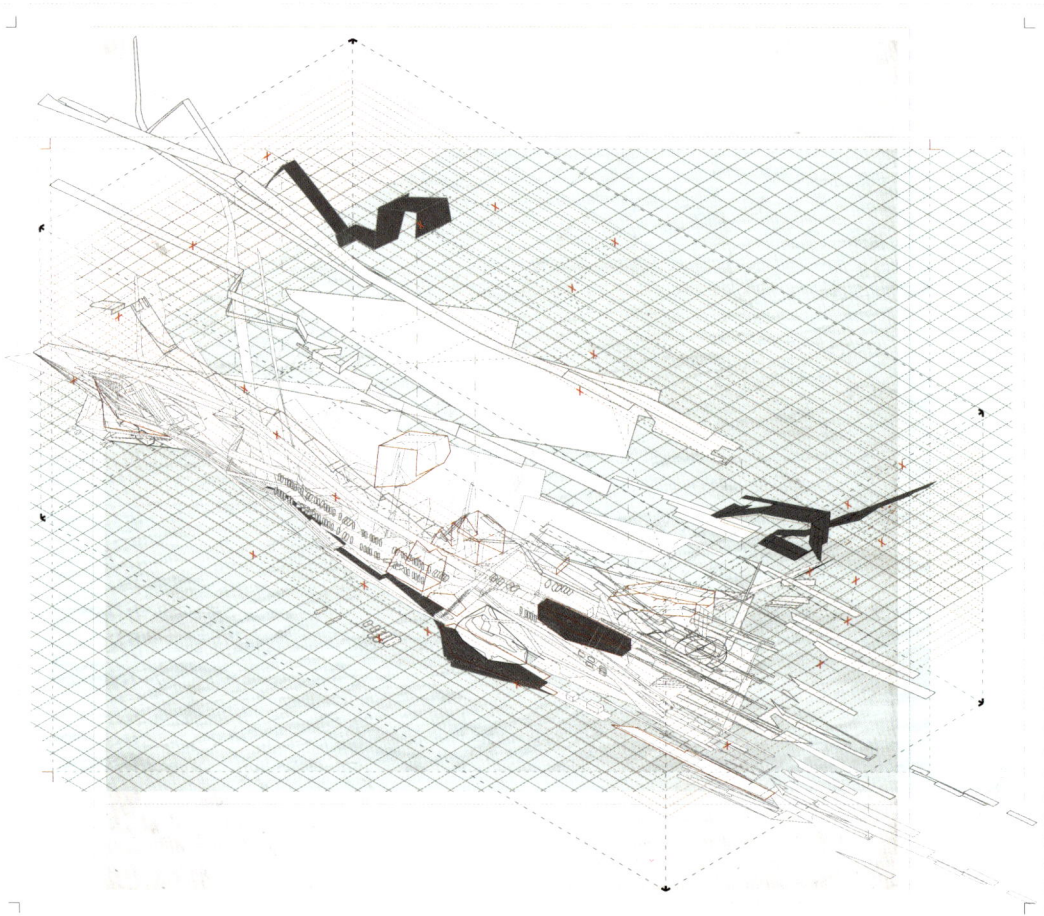

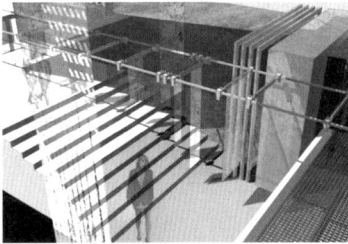

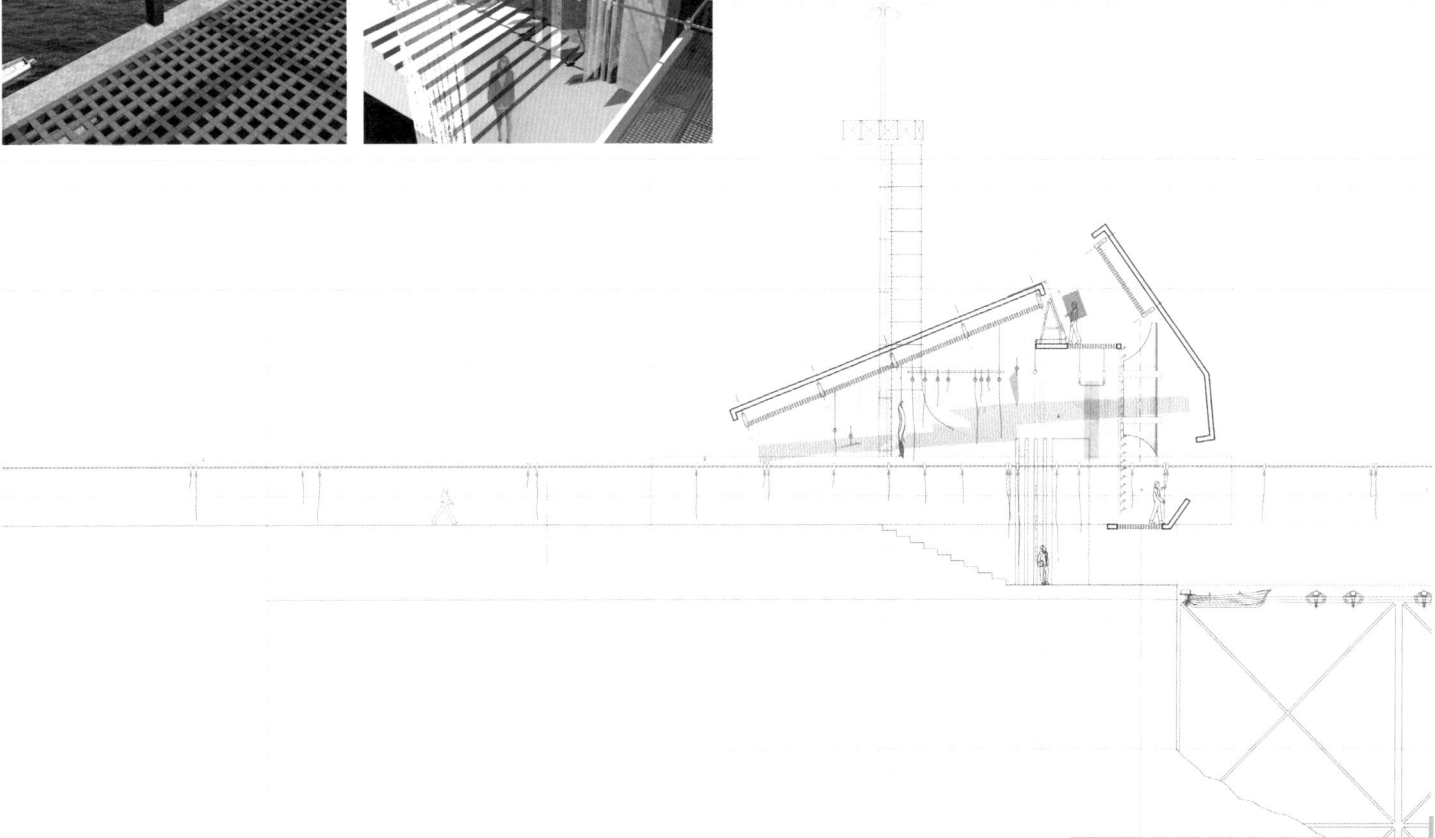

Exchange
Seduction
Suggestion
Stock-Exchange
Wool
Fish
Bread
Granite

Nirupa Puliyel

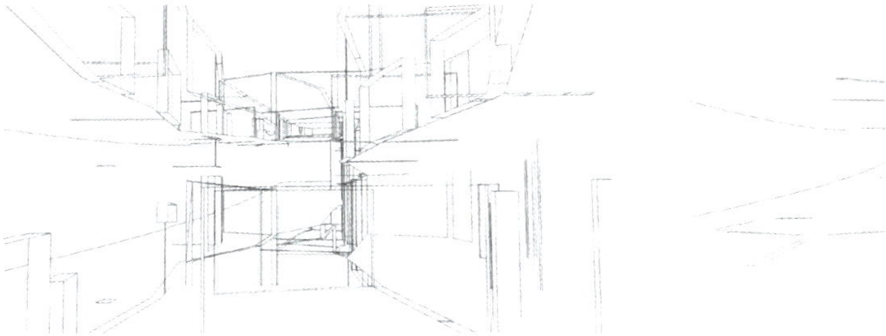

structure analyze

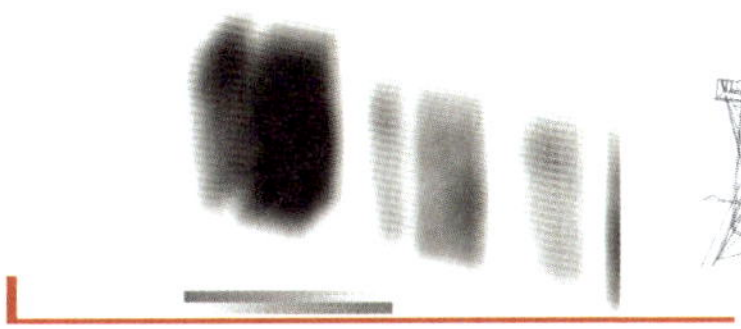

structure analyze

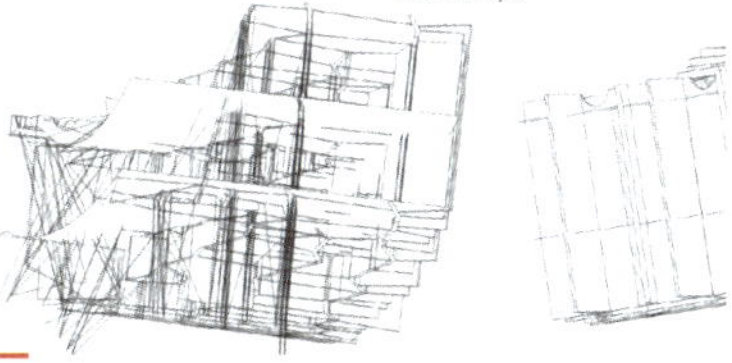

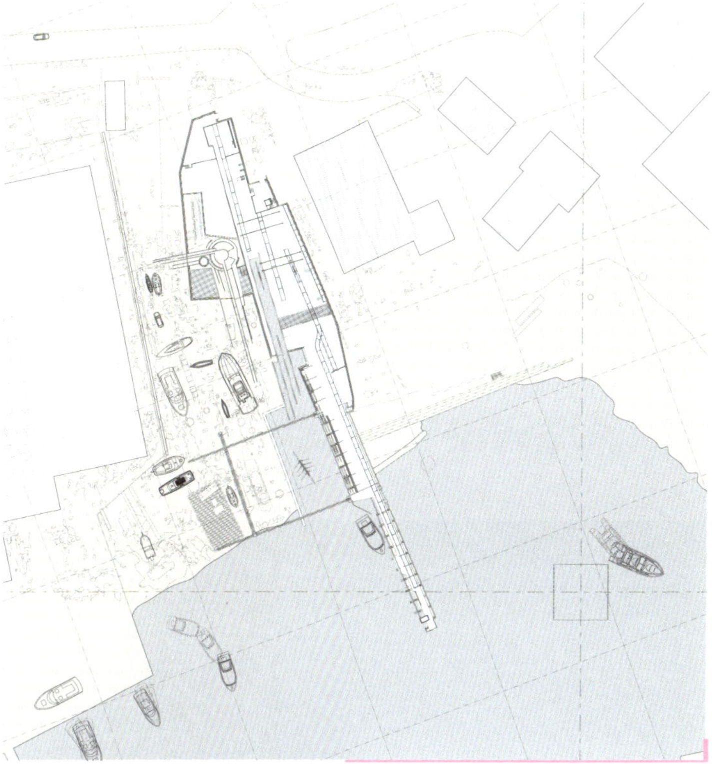

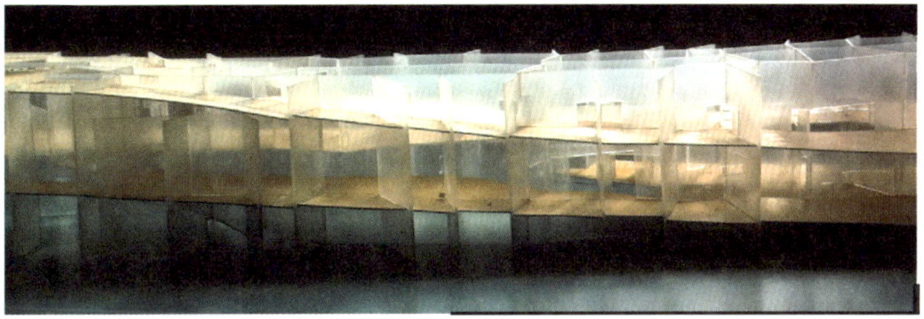

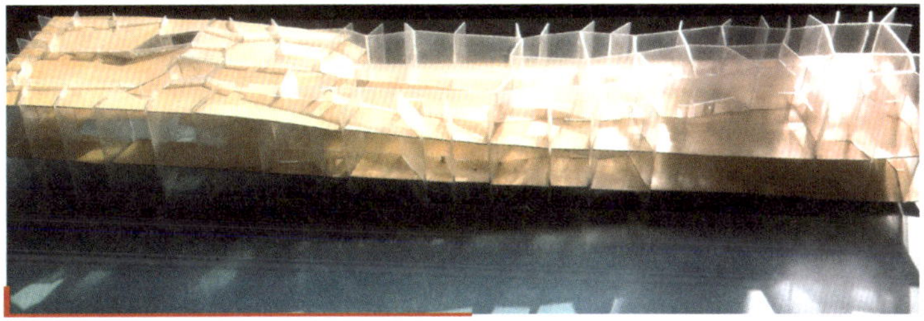

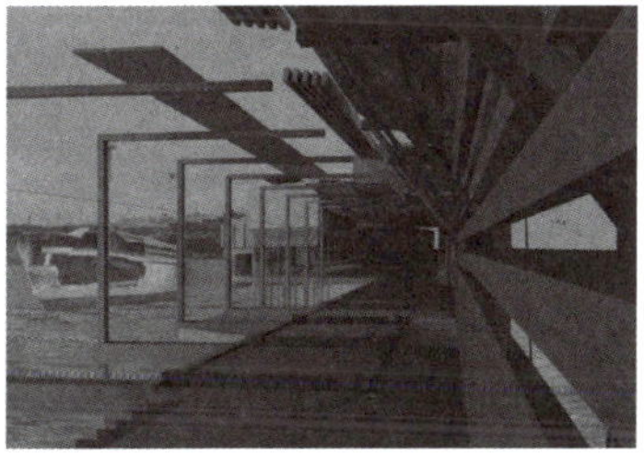

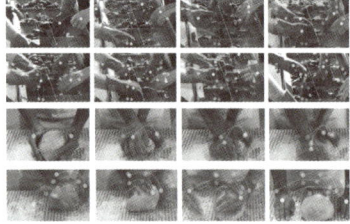

HYDROLOGY HOUSING

Anirudh Sood

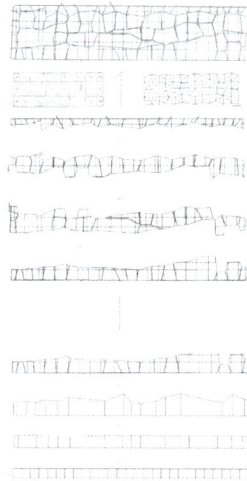

existing public spaces
railway tracks
G1 Fishmarket
G2 Bread market
G3 Linen market
G4 Stone Market
existing location of
mussel farms
municipal proposal for
mussel growing zones
municipal plan for
expansion of ports

scale 1:20,000

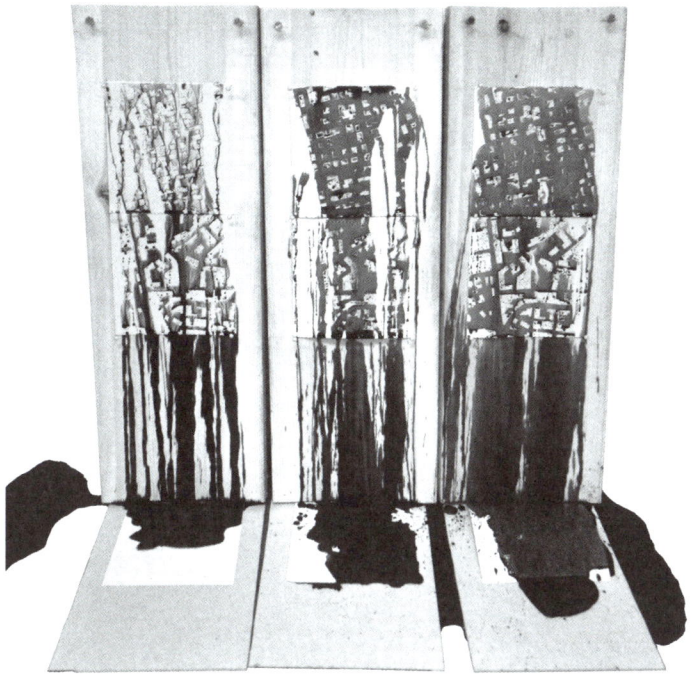

CRUMPLED SHEETS

Mohsen Najafian

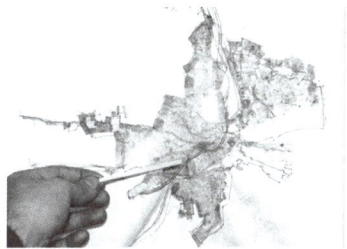

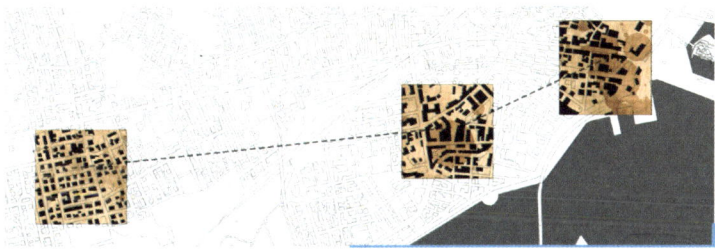

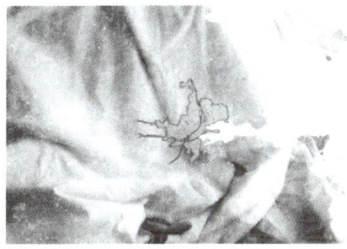

Memory [of Sacred Springs]

Glassworks
Museums
Garden
Water
Bath-House

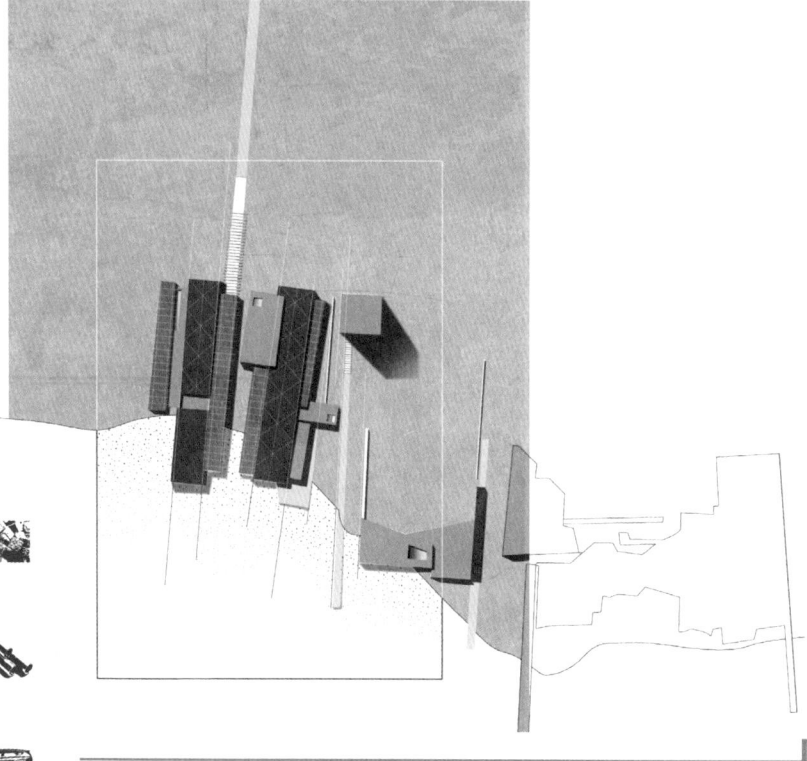

HAND BASINS AND
WATER TEMPLES

Ruth Marsh

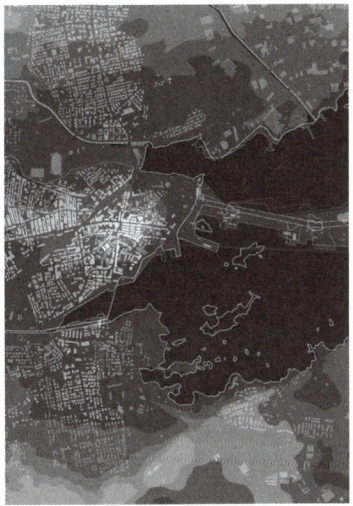

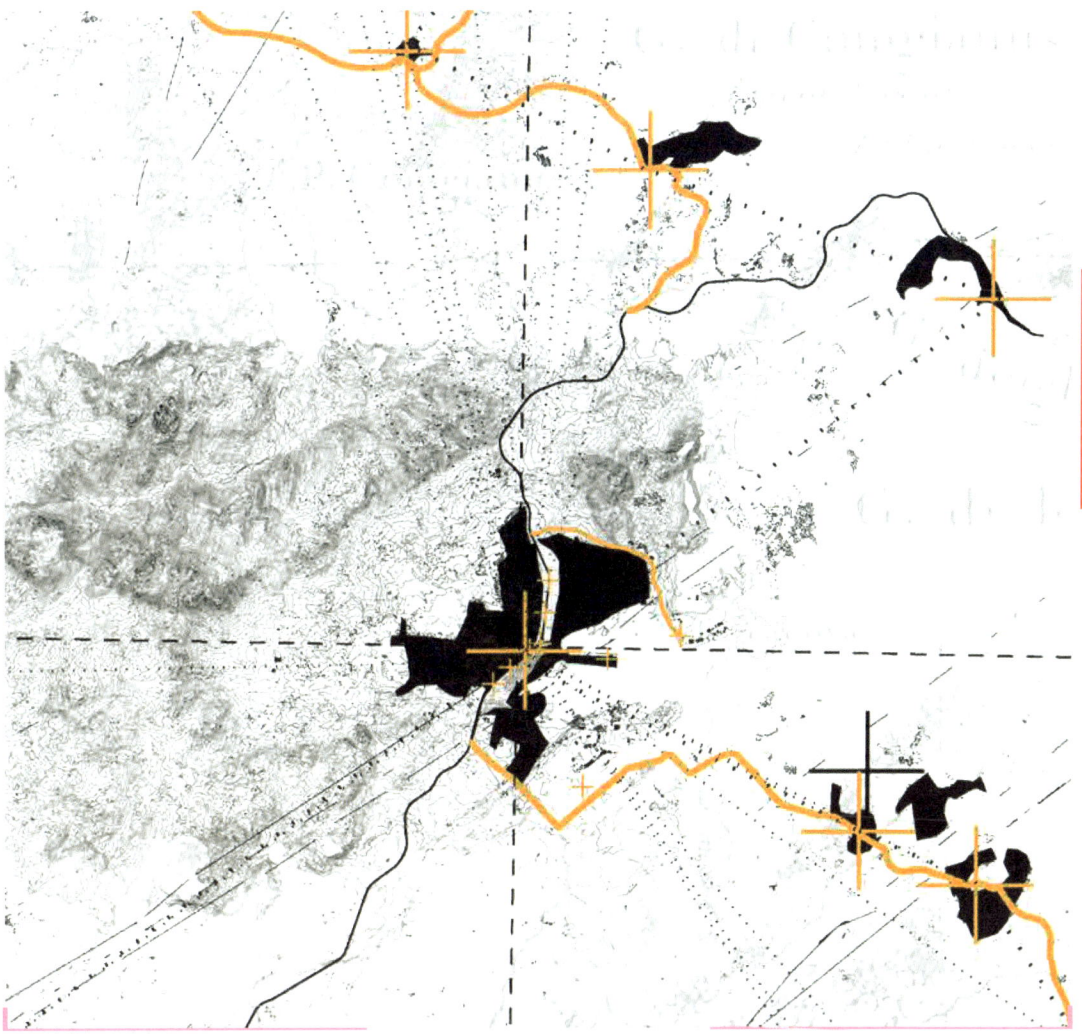

Gesture
Confidence
Hauntology
City Hall
Civic
Offices

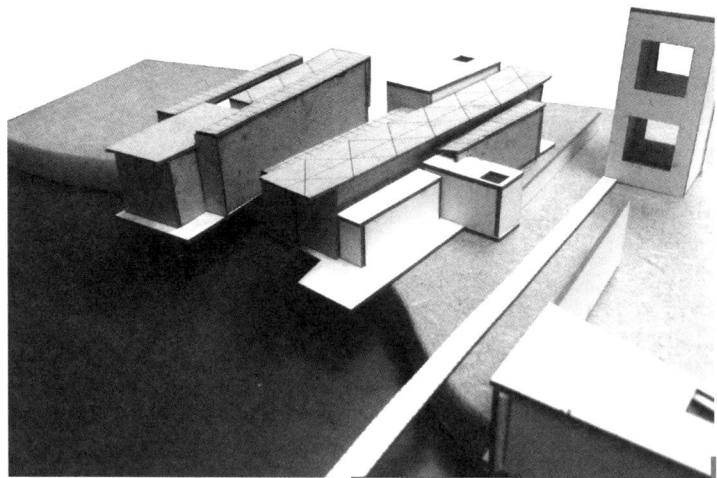

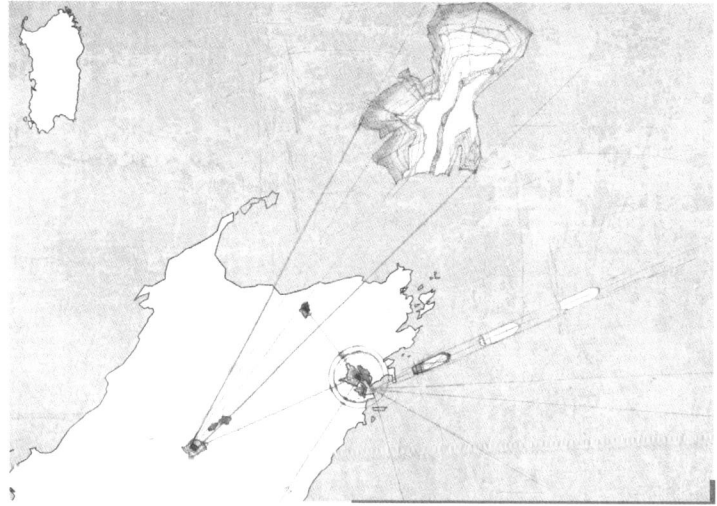

(Tina) Boya Zhang

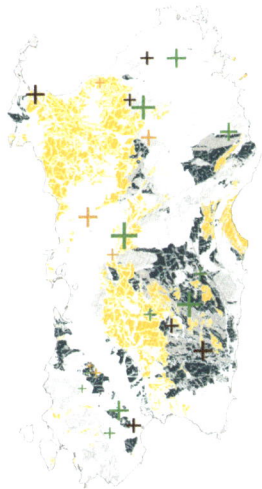

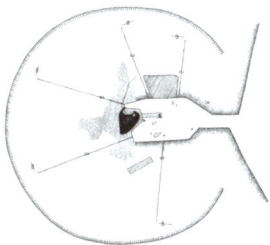

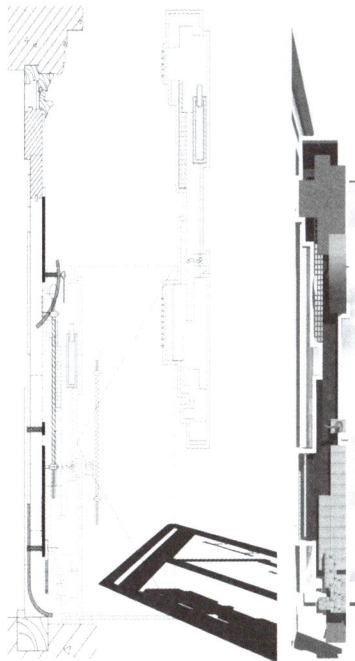

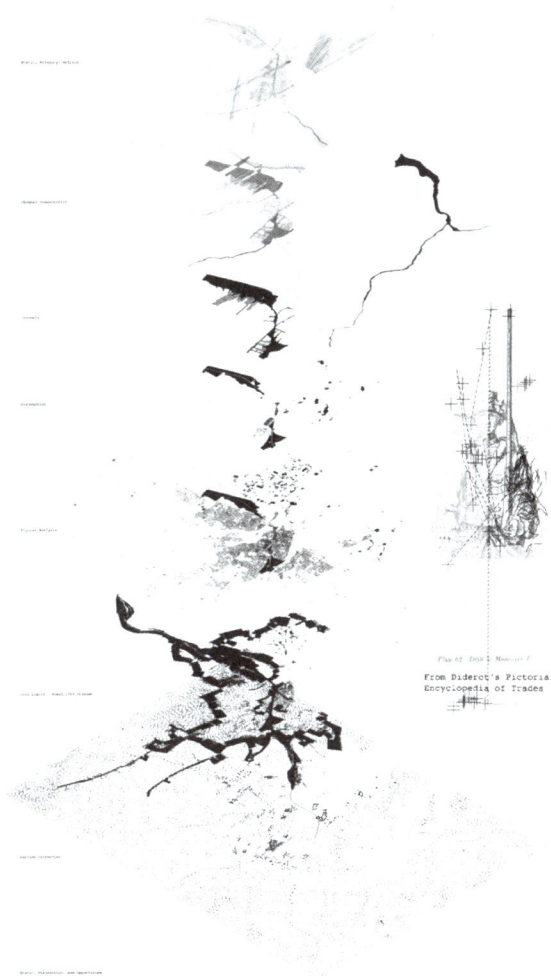

From Diderot's Pictorial
Encyclopedia of Trades

IMPERMEABLE SURFACES AND
FERTILE FISSURES

Lynda Zein

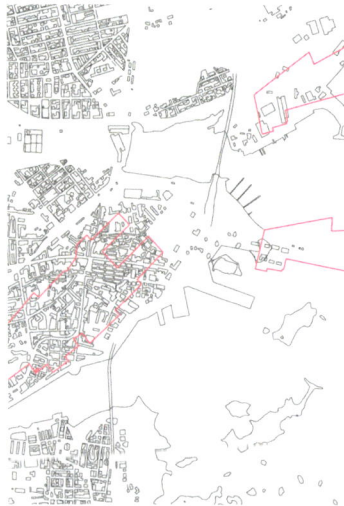

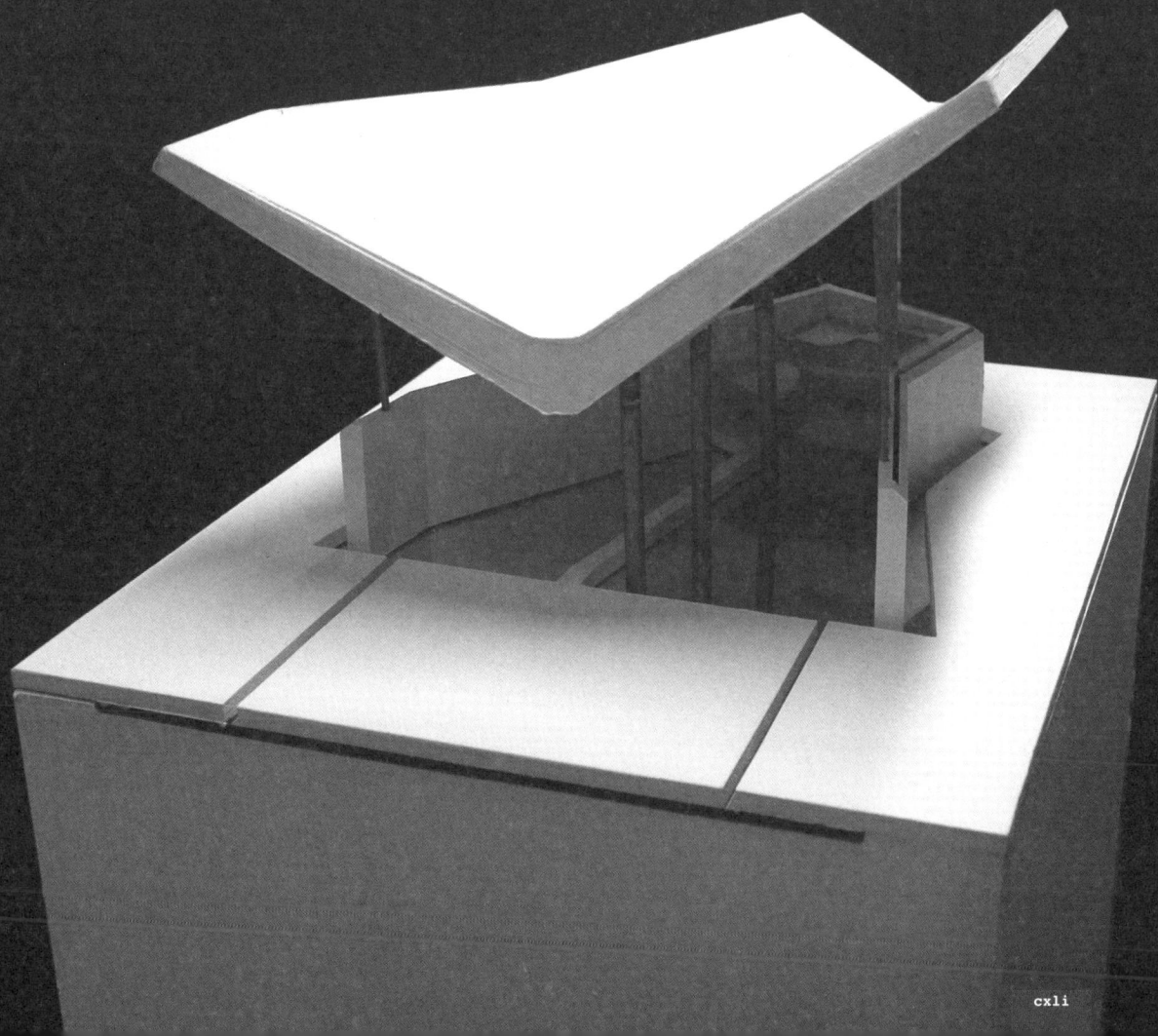

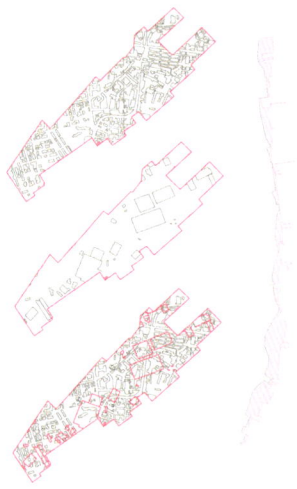

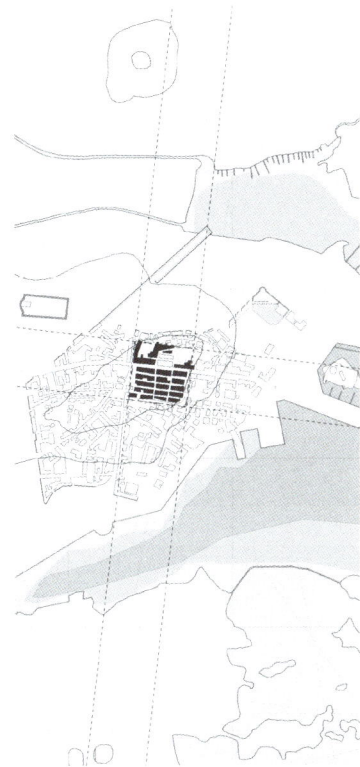

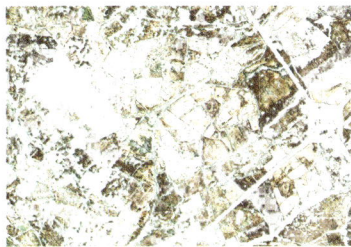

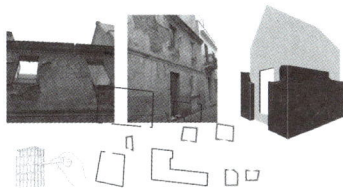

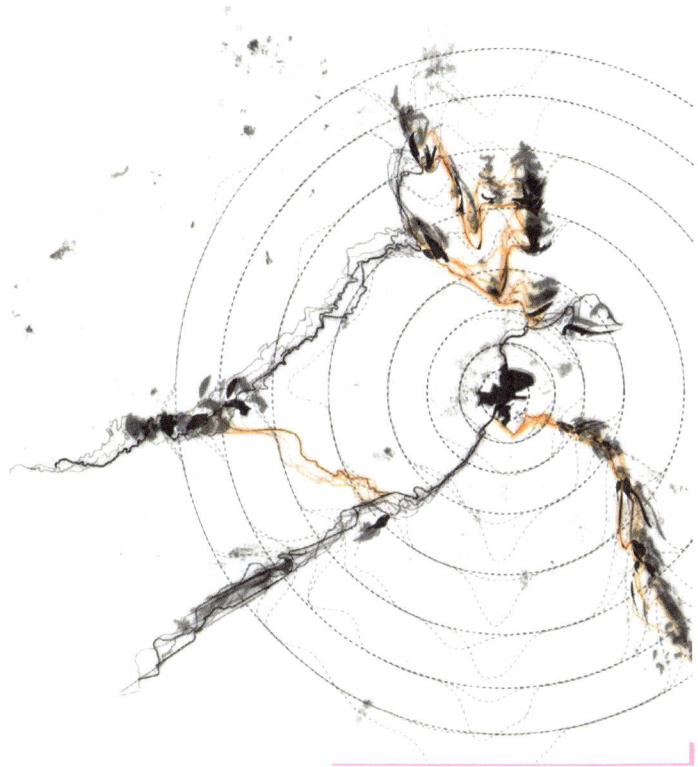

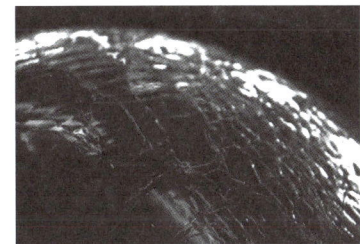

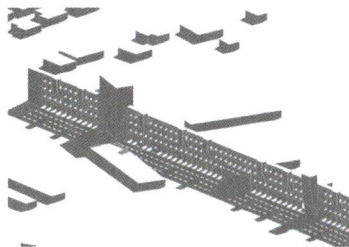

LAW OF THE LAND

No Man's Land
Open Rank
Law Courts
Library
Chambers

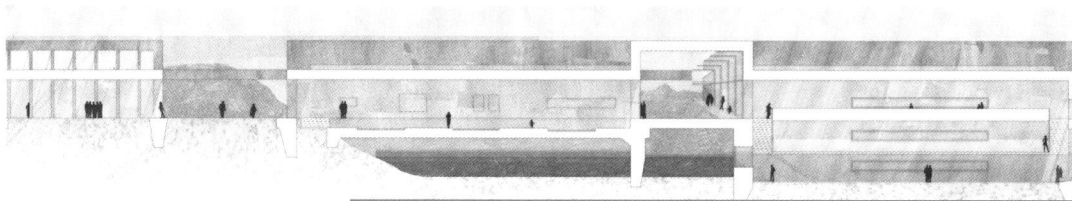

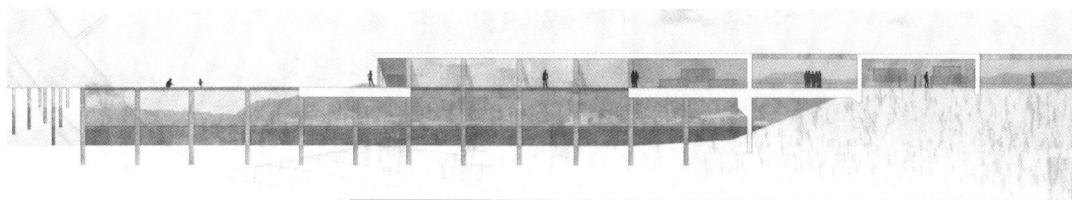

Rachel Stancliffe

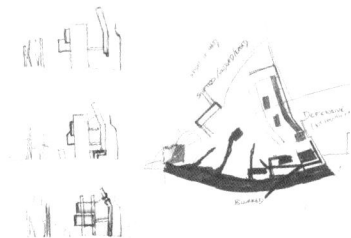

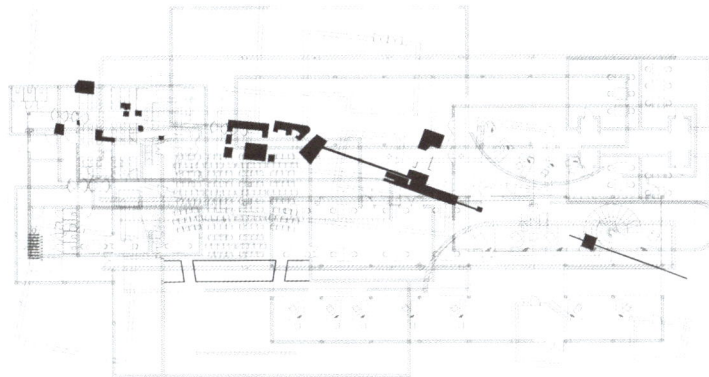

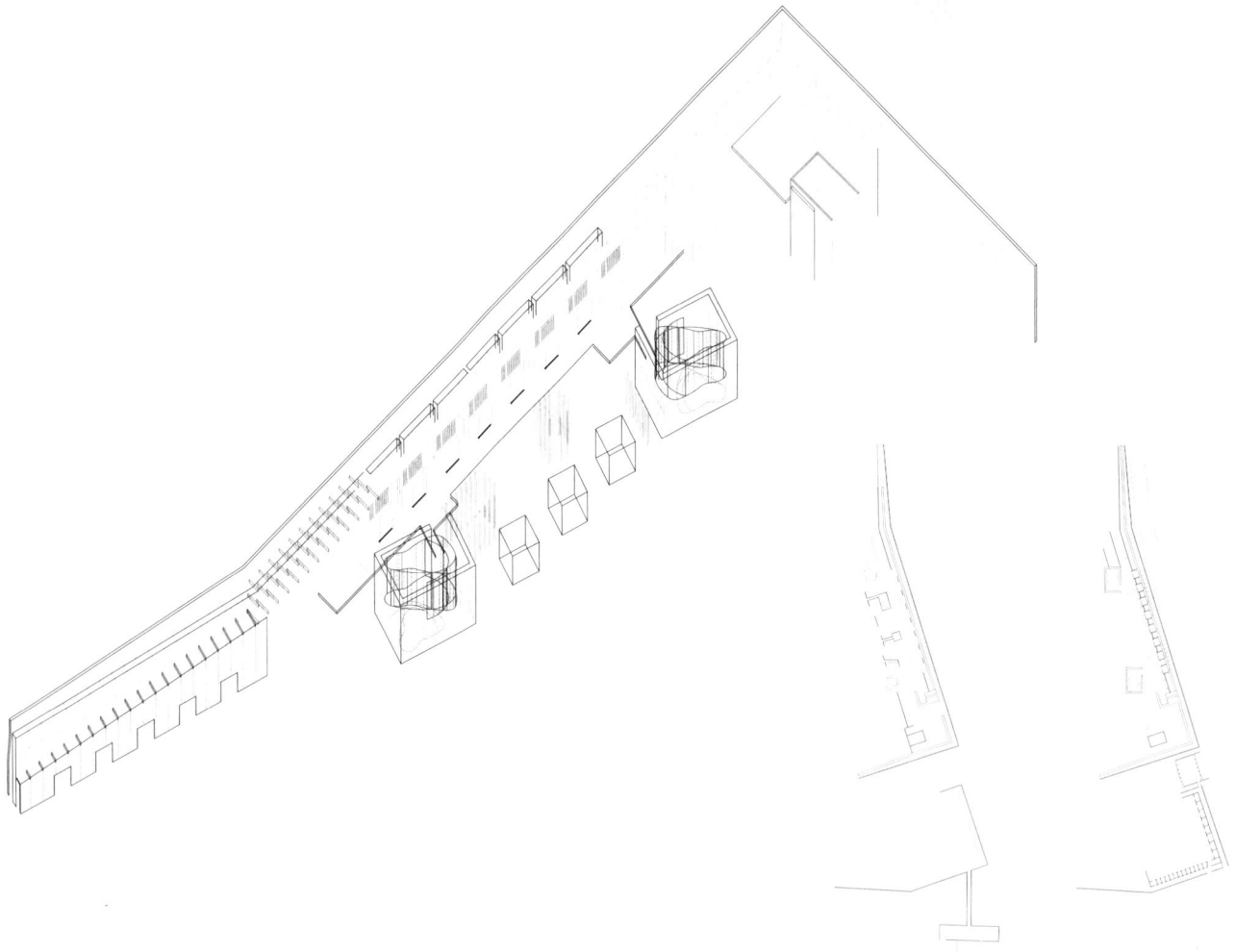

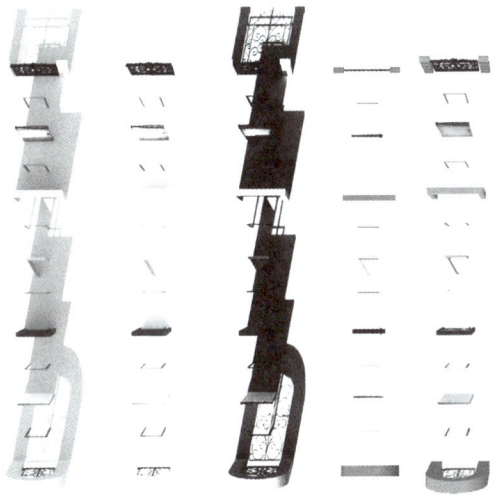

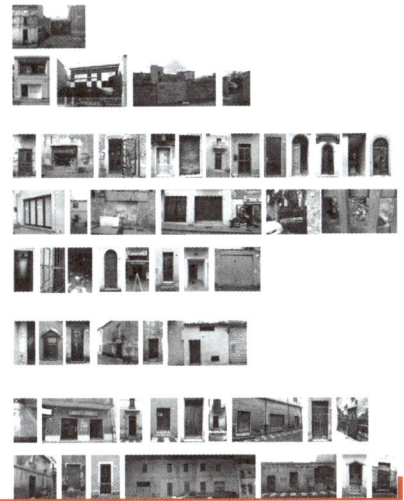

Horizons
Respite

Water
Filtration
View Point
Chapel
Cafe
Playpark

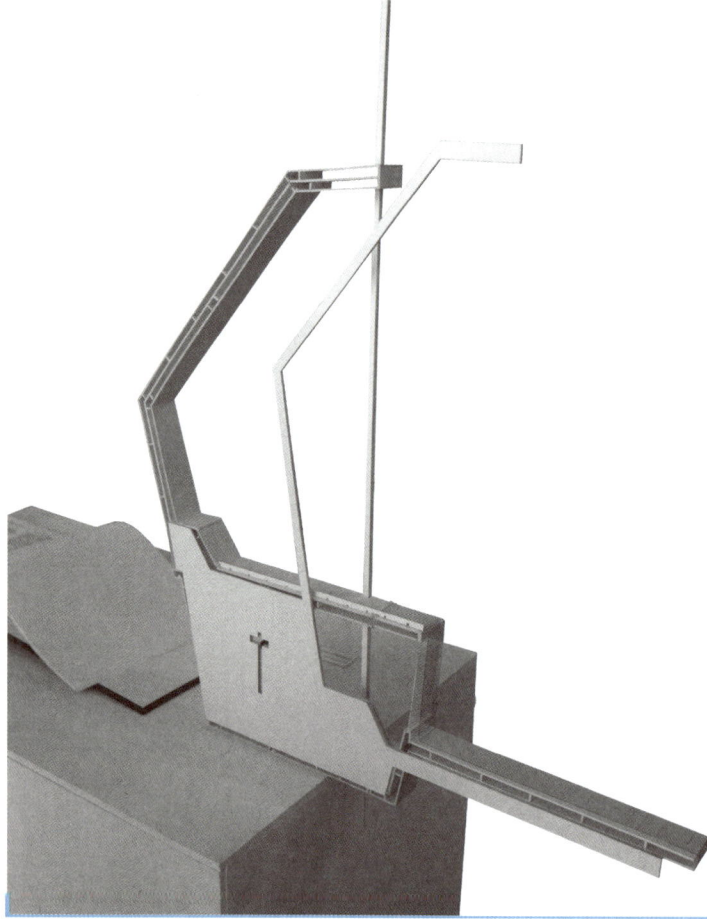

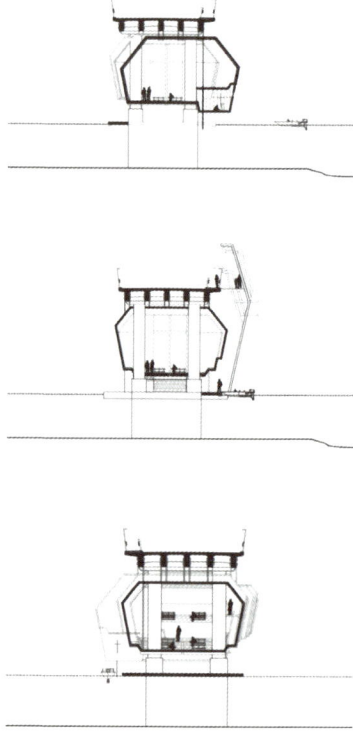

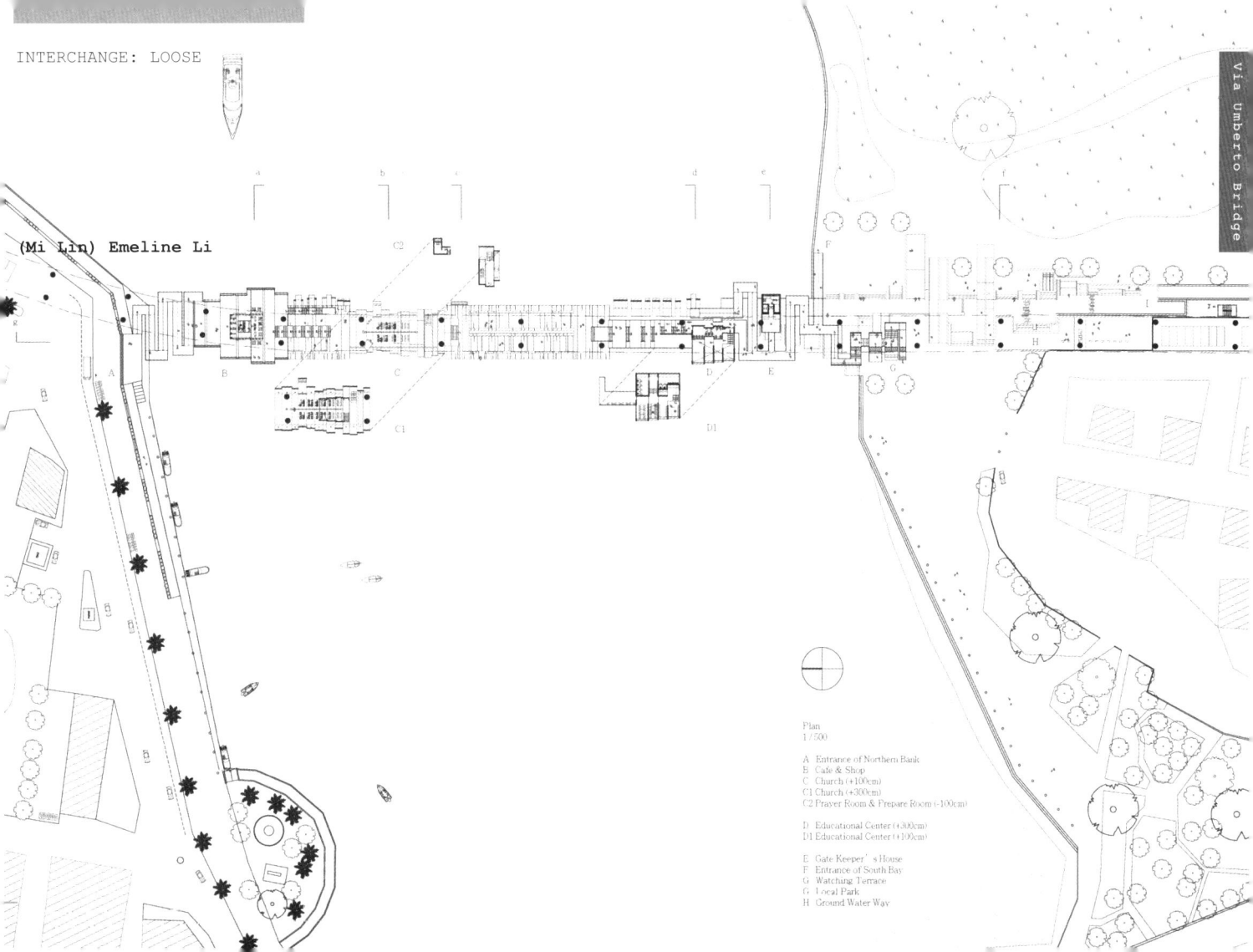

INTERCHANGE: LOOSE

(Mi Lin) Emeline Li

Plan
1/500

A Entrance of Northern Bank
B Cafe & Shop
C Church (+100cm)
C1 Church (+300cm)
C2 Prayer Room & Prepare Room (-100cm)

D Educational Center (+300cm)
D1 Educational Center (+100cm)

E Gate Keeper's House
F Entrance of South Bay
G Watching Terrace
G Local Park
H Ground Water Way

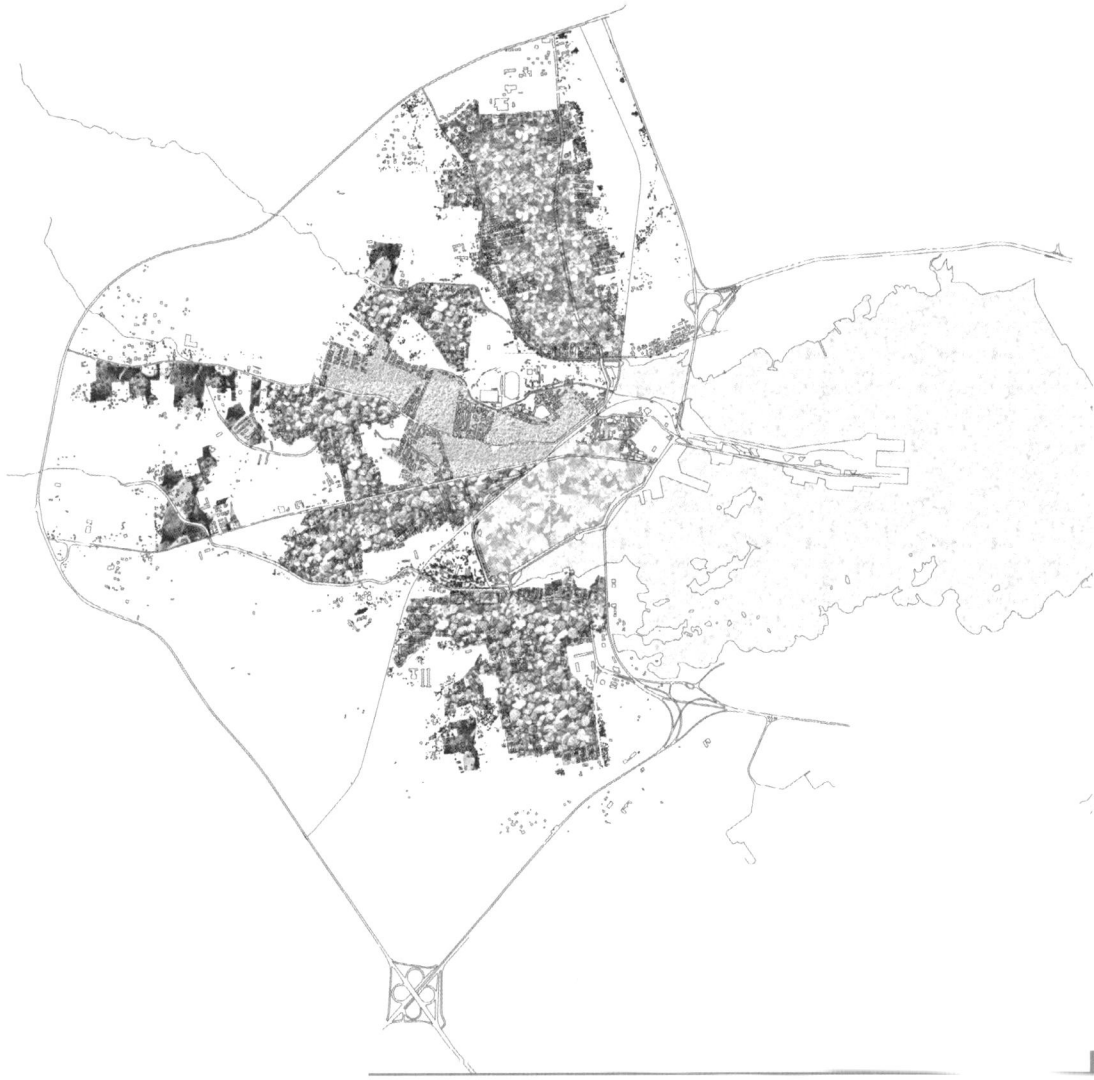

Play
Proportion
Time

Cabinet Maker
Tourist Tower
Sports School

Play
Proportion
Time

Cabinet Maker
Tourist Tower
Sports School

Memory [of Sacred
Springs]

Bath-House
Metal Works

[DIS]PLAYING THE FIELD

Scott Wallace

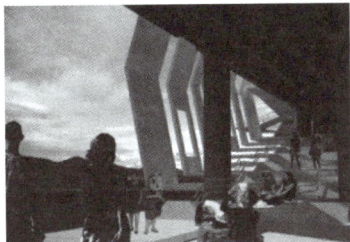

[DIS]PLAYING THE FIELD

SUBSIDING MINDS AND
FLOATING LANDSCAPE

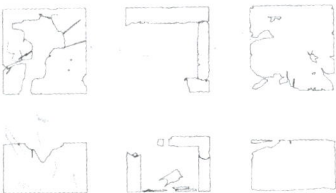

Siyu Wang

Barbara Swierc

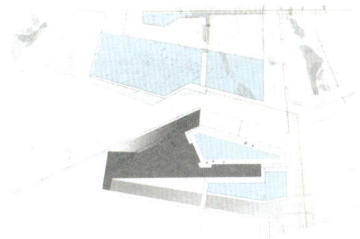

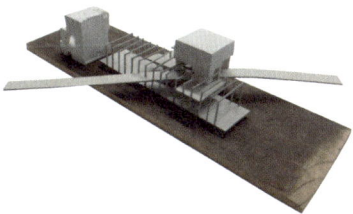

touring line (according
to existing roads)

touring line (subjective
and random)

link between the two ar-
chitectural interventions

echos

sequence of the brochure
arrangement

+   echos of specific places

icon for *FURNITURE MAKER*

icon for *TOURISM BROCHURE*

points of an endless grid

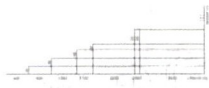

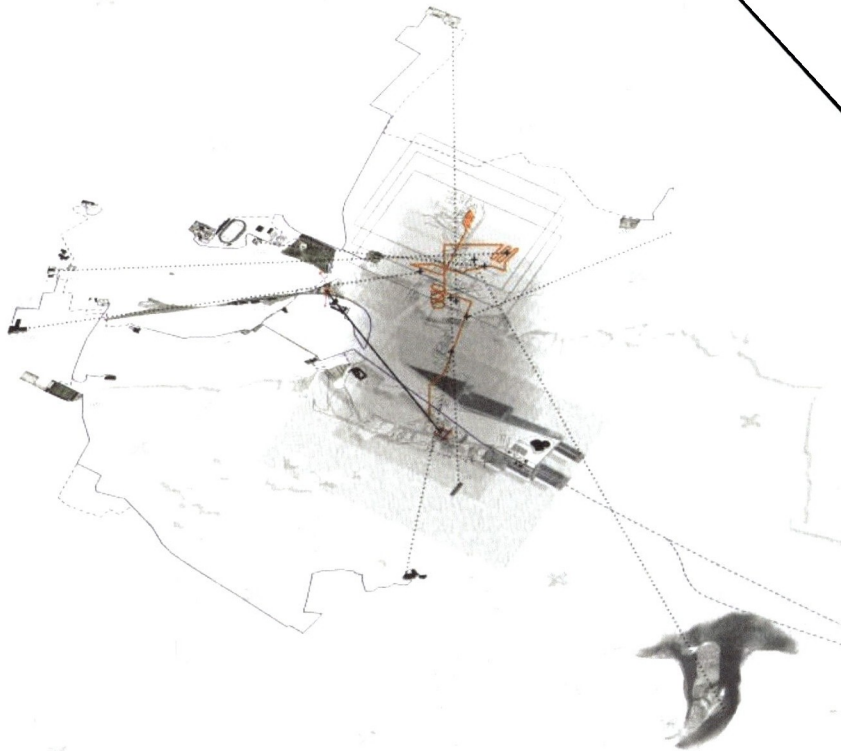

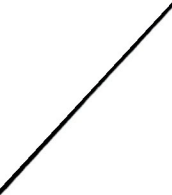

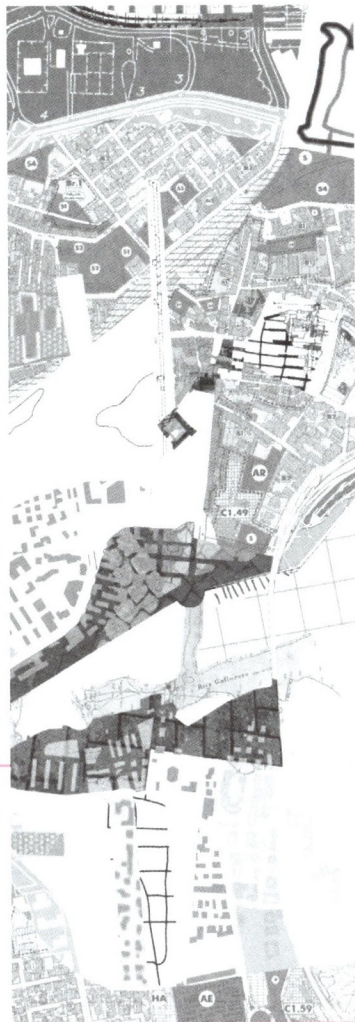

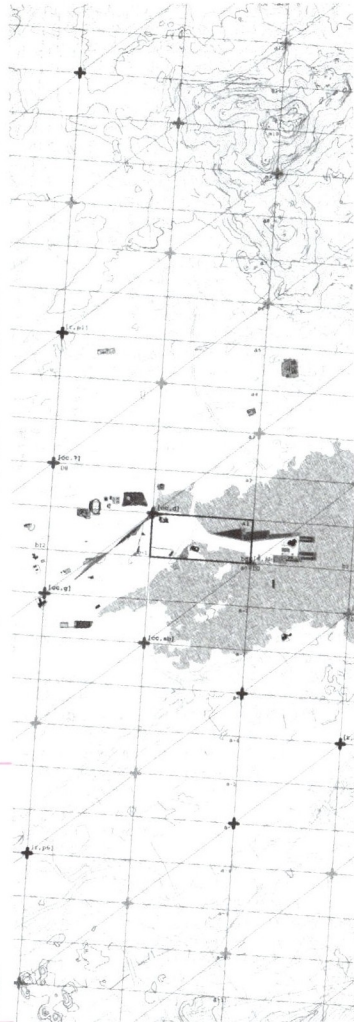

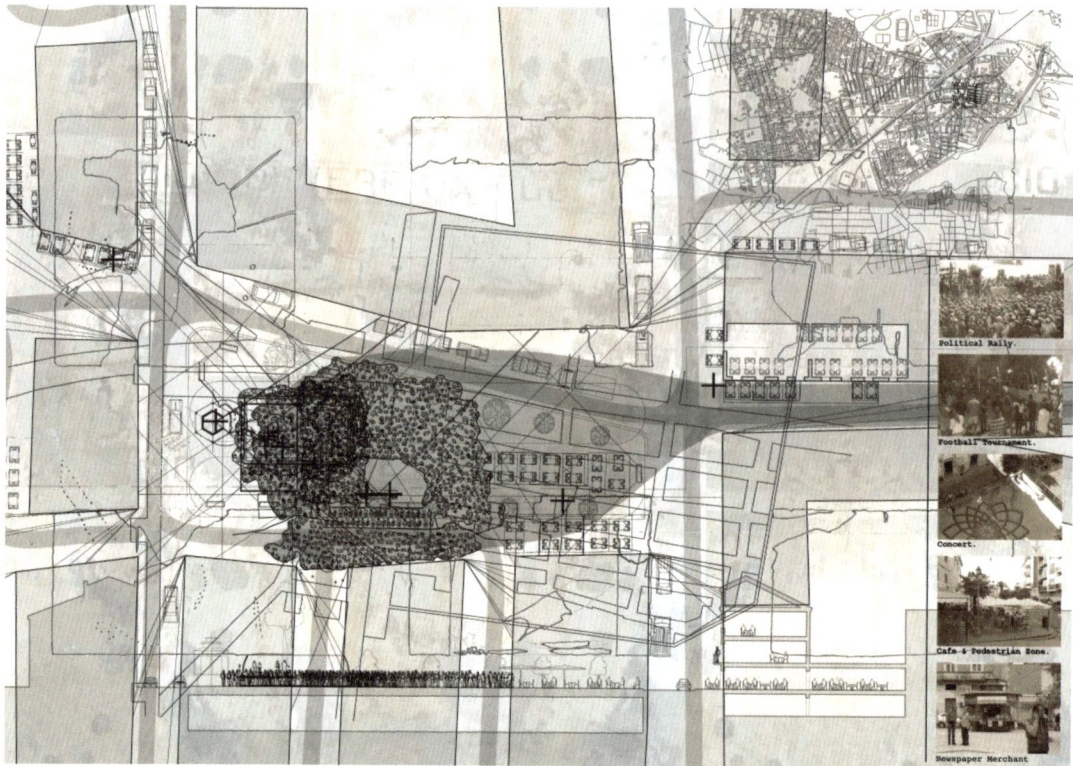

Political Rally.

Football Tournament.

Concert.

Concert.

Cafe & Pedestrian Zone.

Newspaper Merchant

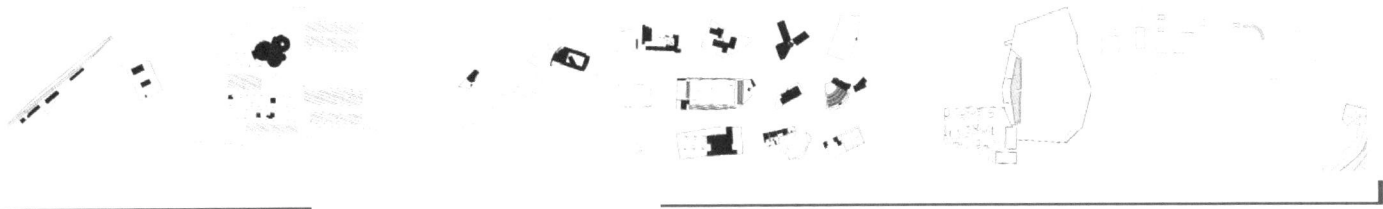

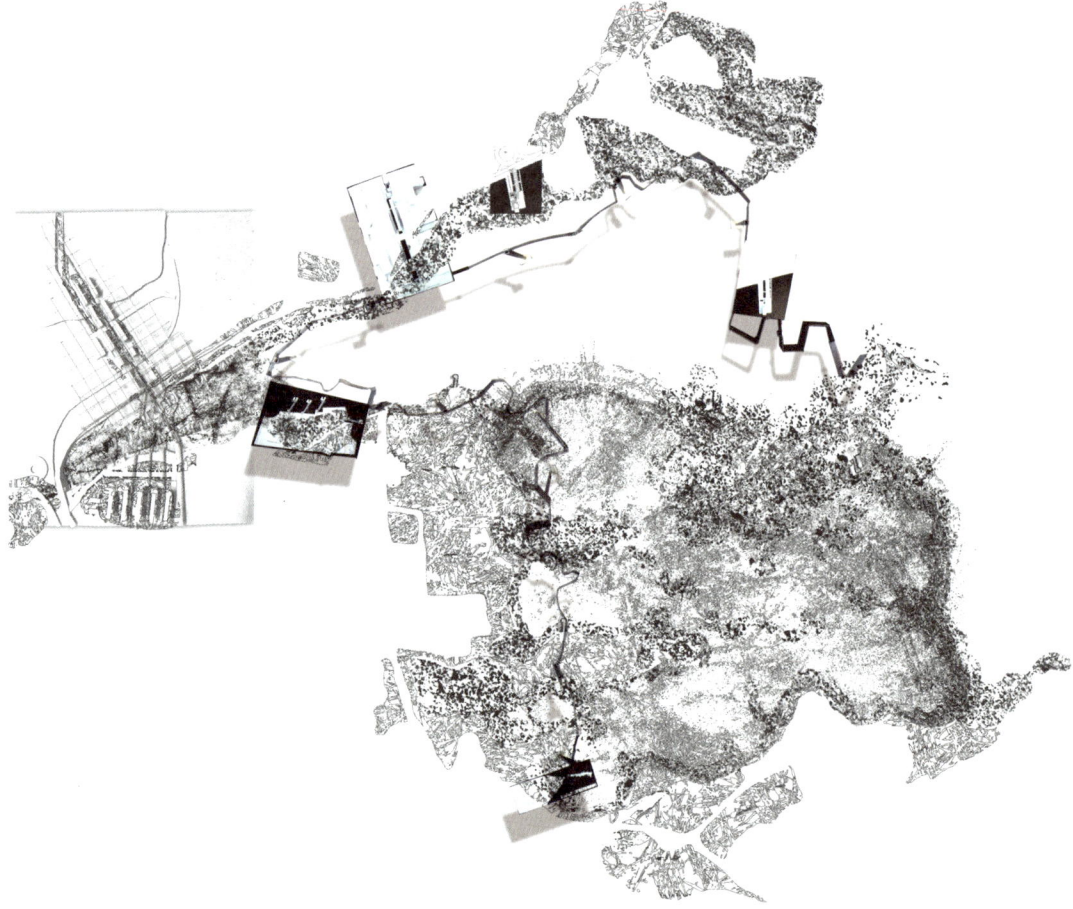

Prosperity
Detritus
Dwelling

Housing
Workshops
Public Space
Theatre
Water
Filtration

Caterina Mendolicchio

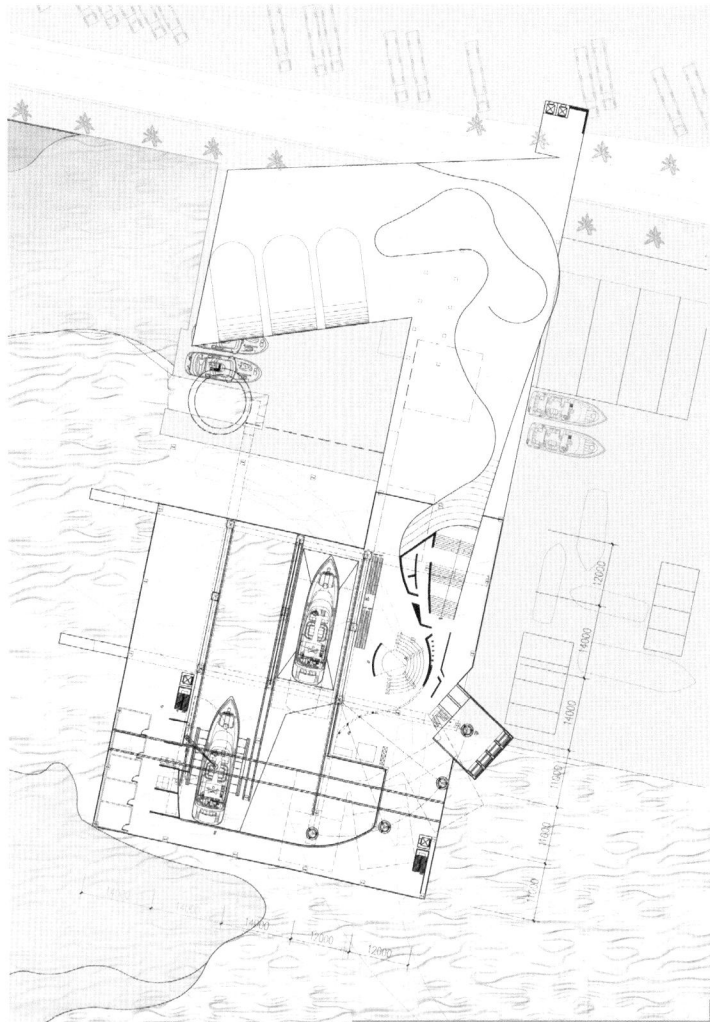

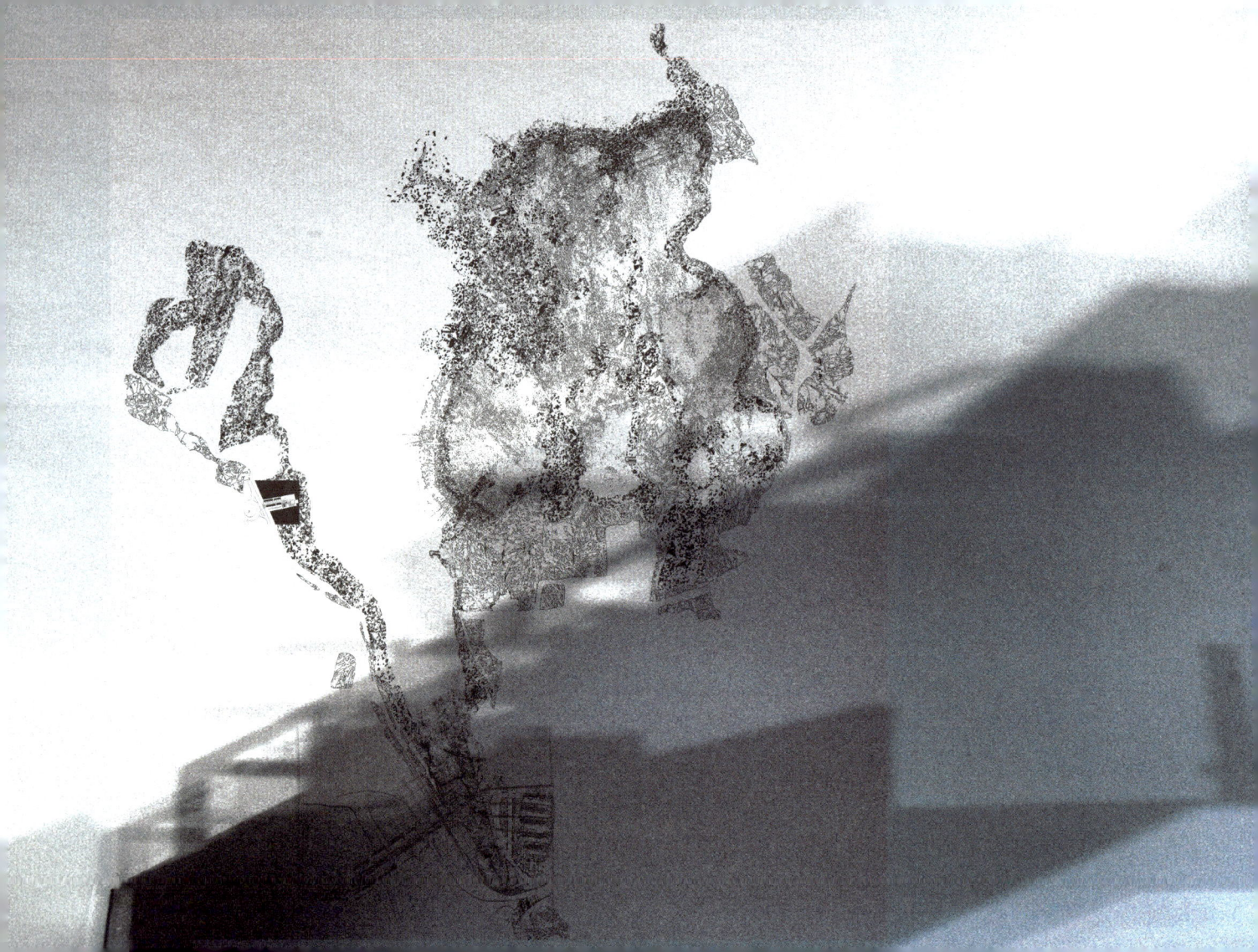

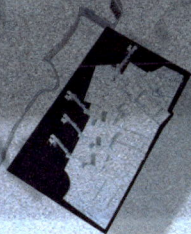

Architectural Initiation

The intention of this research-led design practice is not to represent specific reality, but to construct with knowledge. In correlation with the manifold aspects of our environment, each project is ultimately a unique instance beyond context, but rooted in a deep and informative understanding of its location, proposed activities and projected transformative influences. The architecture is not the expression of research but its foundation, the idea that originates it, the essence discovered in close observations and realized through imaginative capacities. This process demands an awakened view of the social and economical forces active around us as well as the movement in nature and its creating forces. Through such an awakened view, manifested in animated drawings and other forms of representation, our cities could be seen anew.

In the current state of affairs, a conflict between ideas and reality and the separation we experience from the world "out there" further accentuate the rupture between cities and the environment. It is through finding the essence in both natural phenomena and built historical significations that creative activity makes possible new forms of exchange. This process of finding essence is met through experience of one's own understanding expressed in visual terms of what lays beyond the reality in front of us, while developing the skills to make new reality— solid, informed and defined— that can stand out in the world. While pure experience is reality without the

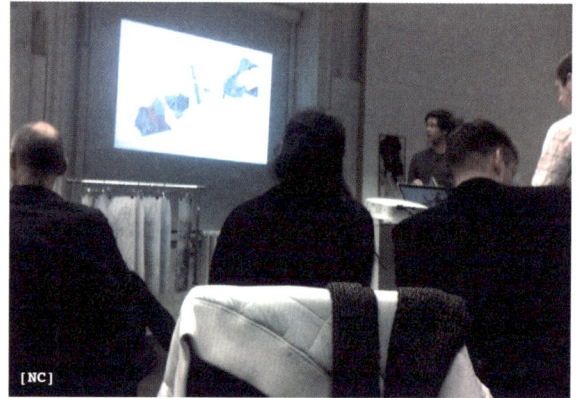

Facoltà di Architettura
Universita degli Studi di Sassari

THE UNIVERSITY *of* EDINBURGH
Edinburgh College of Art

idea, and science works with the idea disconnected from phenomenological reality, this architectural narration is potentially the realm between the two where the character of ideas' essence is used to form new sensory territories.

Architectural tools used for active observations— finding traces on the land, in antiquity and of metropolitan originations— lift and suspend the present into a place where both past and future exist. The work can then be conceptually conceived, providing a positive apparatus for independent practice.

The projects approach the full investigation that brings out the expression of an entire aspect of what they set up for themselves. The architectural project is not 'what is', the present, but what is possible for the future, what could be. It lives in relation to dynamic principles in the environment: nature, the metropolis and the interrelations between them. It is therefore built in relation to the past but not out of the past, with a clear objective on its effect on landscape and urbanity.

The independence of the activity of play departs beyond what is given in the world, and becomes free; the mark of subjectivity in reality in turn validates subjectivity with objective reality. Similarly, a free and exploratory environment is necessary for a threefold relation between affirmation of imagination, initiation, and reevaluation. This is the valuable, constant and free movement between creative, subjective acts and a rigorous reading of context. The work is evaluated at once according to what is brought to the site, and in

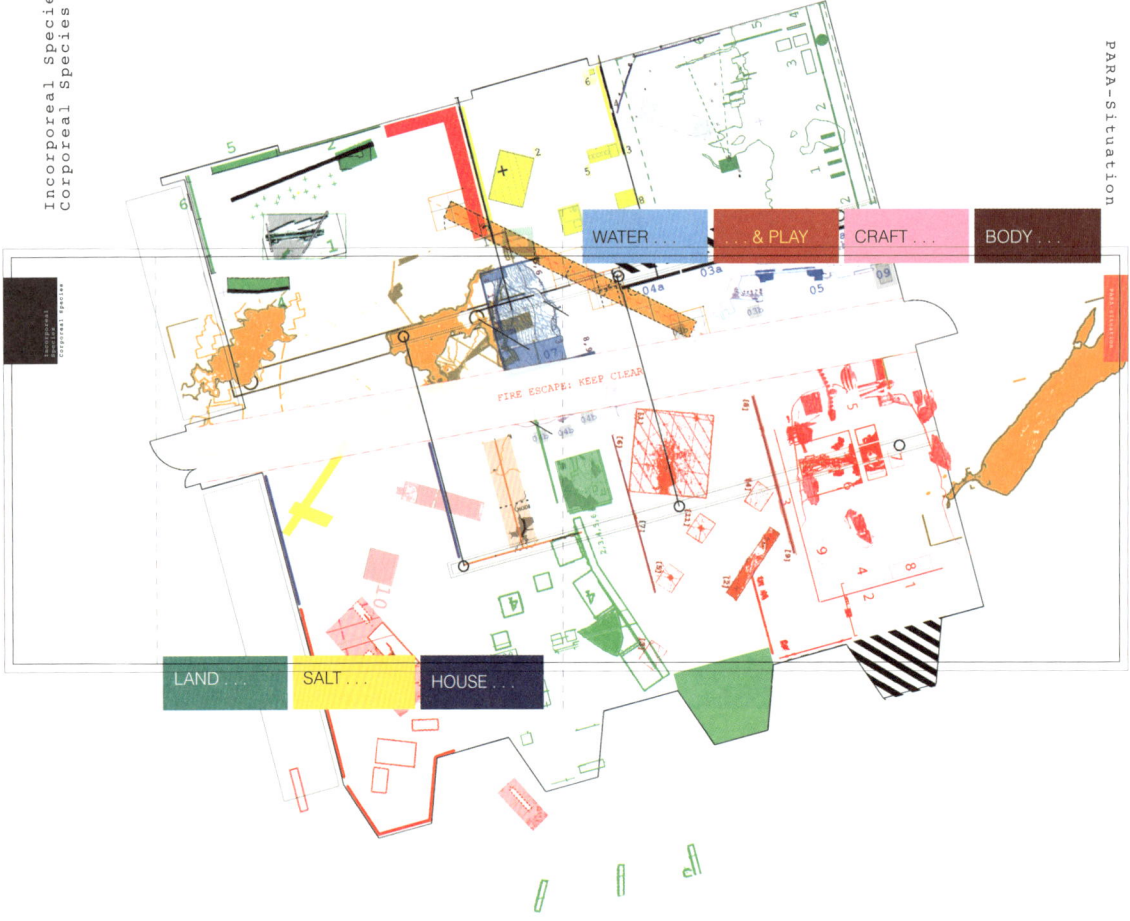

WATER . . .   . . . & PLAY   CRAFT . . .   BODY . . .

FIRE ESCAPE: KEEP CLEAR

LAND . . .   SALT . . .   HOUSE . . .

working within the grounding on which it is based. It is out of its intrinsic connectivity, in dialogical relation not in dialectical relations, that the project's value connects back to the whole, and creates new structural presence— a new sensory reality.

   In finding the "ecosophic object", it is not the idea that takes the form in the sensory world. Rather, it is a sensory phenomenon in the form of idea. We strive for new forms rather than the translation of ideas to familiar forms. Seeing the environment anew through engaging and active research, the creative architectural act bears vision for human activities that fundamentally relate to natural conditions, but go beyond what is offered by the landscape and found in the city—constructing systems of latent relations: "The earth is the living surface that brings force shapes" (Rudolf Steiner, 1914). And, while connecting to local ecological truths, the project can characterize forces, uplifting reality in the Initiation of Forms grounded in the structural integrity of new compositions.

(YH)

THE [LOVING] METRO

Bibliography

Agamben Giorgio, *Profanations*, trans. Jeff Fort (New York: Zone Books, 2007).

Agamben, Giorgio, Homo Sacer, *Sovereign Power and Bare Life*, (Stanford: Stanford University Press, 1998)

Agamben, Giorgio, *Infancy And History, On The Destruction of Experience*, trans. Liz Heron (Verso, London-New York, 2007).

Agamben, Giorgio, *Means Without End, Notes on Politics*, trans. Vincenzo Binetti and Cesare Casarino (Minneapolis: University of Minnesota Press, Minneapolis, 2000).

Agamben, Giorgio, *Metropolis*, translated from Audio files by AriannaBove, The European Graduate School, March 17 2007, http://www.egs.edu/faculty/giorgio-agamben/articles/metropolis/

Agamben, Giorgio, *Potentialities, Collected Essays in Philosophy*, ed. and trans. Daniel Heller-Roazen (Stanford University Press, California, 1999).

Agamben, Giorgio, Stanzas, *Word And Phantasm In Western Culture*, trans. Ronald L. Martinez (Minnesota: University Of Minnesota Press, 1993).

Agamben, Giorgio, *State of Exception*, trans. Kevin Attel (University of Chicago Press, Chicago, 2005).

Agamben, Giorgio, *The Coming Community*, trans. Michael Hardt (Minneapolis: University of Minnesota Press, 2007).

Agamben, Giorgio, *What is an Apparatus? and Other Essays*, Trans. David Kishik and Stefan Pedatella, (Stanford California: Stanford University Press, 2009).

Agrest, Diana and Mario Gandelsonas, 'Semiotics and Architecture: Ideological Consumption or Theoretical Work,' in *Theorizing A New Agenda For Architecture, An Anthology of Architectural Theory*, 1965-1995, ed. Kate Nesbitt (New York: Princeton Architectural Press, 1996) pp.110-121.

Agrest, Diana, 'Design versus Non-Design,' in *Oppositions Reader, Selected Readings from A Journal for Ideas and Criticism in Architecture*, 1973-1984, ed. K. Michael Hays (New York: Princeton Architectural Press,1998) pp.331-354.

Agrest, Diana, 'Representation as Articulation between Theory and Practice,' in Allen, Stan, *Essays, Practice, Architecture, Technique and Representation* (Amsterdam: G+B Arts International, 2000) pp.163-177.

Agrest, Diana, *Architecture from Without* (Cambridge, MA: MIT Press, 1991).

Allen, Stan, *Essays, Practice, Architecture, Technique and Representation* (Amsterdam: G+B Arts International, Netherlands, 2000).

Allen, Stan, Piranesi's Campo Marzio: An Experimental Design, in *Assemblage*, No. 10 Dec. 1989, (Cambridge MA: MIT Press, 1989) pp.70-109.

Allen, Stan, Points + Lines, Diagrams and Projects for The City (New York: Princeton Architectural Press, 1999).

Archizoom and Andrea Branzi, *Casabella*, 399, 1975 (Milan: Studio Editoriale Milanese, 1975)

Arendt, Hannah, *The Human Condition* (Chicago: University of Chicago Press, 1998).

Aristotle, Book Q, *Metaphysics*, trans., John Warrington, Everyman's Library (Letchworth: The Aldine Press, 1956)

Aureli, Pier Vittorio, *More and More about Less and Less: Notes Towards a History of Nonfigurative Architecture*, Log 16, ed. Cynthia Davidson (New York: Anycorp, 2009)

Aureli, Pier Vittorio, Unger's Berlin and Green Archipelago, 'Toward the Archipelago,' in *Log 11* ed. Cynthia Davidson (New York: Anycorp, 2008)

Auster, Paul, *New York Trilogy* (London: Faber and Faber, 1987).

Badiou, Alain, with Nicolas Trong, In *Praise of Love*, trans. Peter Bush (London: Serpent's Tail; Profile Books, 2012)

Baird, George, *The Space of Appearance*, (Cambridge MA: MIT Press, 2003)

Bataille, Georges, *The Encyclopaedia Acephalica*, ed. Alastair Brotchie (London: Atlas Press, 1995).

Bataille, Georges, The Notion of Expenditure, in *The Bataille Reader*, ed. Fred Botting and Scott Wilson (London: Blackwell, 1997) pp. 167-187

Bateson, Gregory, *Steps to an Ecology of Mind* (Chicago: University of Chicago Press, 2000)

Baudrillard, Jean, The Rise of the Object: The End of Culture, in *Mass, Identity, Architecture, Architectural Writings of Jean Baudrillard*, ed. Francesco Proto, (London: Wiley, 2006) pp.95-121.

Benjamin, Walter, *Illuminations*, ed. Hannah Arendt, (London: Fontana Press, 1992).

Benjamin, Walter, *Reflections, Essays, Aphorisms, Autobiographical Writings*, trans. Edmund Jephcott, ed. Peter Demetz (New York: Schocken Books, 1986).

Benjamin, Walter, *Understanding Brecht*, trans. Anna Bostock (London: Verso, 1983).

Benjamin, Walter, *Walter Benjamin, Selected Writings*, vol. 2, part 1, 1927-1930, trans. Rodney Livingstone and others, ed. Michael W. Jennings, Howard Eiland and Gary Smith (Cambridge, MA: The Belknap Press of Harvard University Press, 2005).

Bhabha, Homi, *The Location of Culture* (Abingdon: Routledge, 2005)

Blanchot, Maurice, *The Station Hill Blanchot Reader, Fiction and Literary Essays* (New York: Station Hill Press, 1999).

Bibliography

Agamben Giorgio, *Profanations*, trans. Jeff Fort (New York: Zone Books, 2007).

Agamben, Giorgio, Homo Sacer, *Sovereign Power and Bare Life*, (Stanford: Stanford University Press, 1998)

Agamben, Giorgio, *Infancy And History, On The Destruction of Experience*, trans. Liz Heron (Verso, London-New York, 2007).

Agamben, Giorgio, *Means Without End, Notes on Politics*, trans. Vincenzo Binetti and Cesare Casarino (Minneapolis: University of Minnesota Press, Minneapolis, 2000).

Agamben, Giorgio, *Metropolis*, translated from Audio files by AriannaBove, The European Graduate School, March 17 2007, http://www.egs.edu/faculty/giorgio-agamben/articles/metropolis/

Agamben, Giorgio, *Potentialities, Collected Essays in Philosophy*, ed. and trans. Daniel Heller-Roazen (Stanford University Press, California, 1999).

Agamben, Giorgio, Stanzas, *Word And Phantasm In Western Culture*, trans. Ronald L. Martinez (Minnesota: University Of Minnesota Press, 1993).

Agamben, Giorgio, *State of Exception*, trans. Kevin Attel (University of Chicago Press, Chicago, 2005).

Agamben, Giorgio, *The Coming Community*, trans. Michael Hardt (Minneapolis: University of Minnesota Press, 2007).

Agamben, Giorgio, *What is an Apparatus? and Other Essays*, Trans. David Kishik and Stefan Pedatella, (Stanford California: Stanford University Press, 2009).

Agrest, Diana and Mario Gandelsonas, 'Semiotics and Architecture: Ideological Consumption or Theoretical Work,' in *Theorizing A New Agenda For Architecture, An Anthology of Architectural Theory*, 1965-1995, ed. Kate Nesbitt (New York: Princeton Architectural Press, 1996) pp.110-121.

Agrest, Diana, 'Design versus Non-Design,' in *Oppositions Reader, Selected Readings from A Journal for Ideas and Criticism in Architecture*, 1973-1984, ed. K. Michael Hays (New York: Princeton Architectural Press,1998) pp.331-354.

Agrest, Diana, 'Representation as Articulation between Theory and Practice,' in Allen, Stan, *Essays, Practice, Architecture, Technique and Representation* (Amsterdam: G+B Arts International, 2000) pp.163-177.

Agrest, Diana, *Architecture from Without* (Cambridge, MA: MIT Press, 1991).

Allen, Stan, *Essays, Practice, Architecture, Technique and Representation* (Amsterdam: G+B Arts International, Netherlands, 2000).

Allen, Stan, Piranesi's Campo Marzio: An Experimental Design, in *Assemblage*, No. 10 Dec. 1989, (Cambridge MA: MIT Press, 1989) pp.70-109.

Allen, Stan, *Points + Lines, Diagrams and Projects for The City* (New York: Princeton Architectural Press, 1999).

Archizoom and Andrea Branzi, *Casabella*, 399, 1975 (Milan: Studio Editoriale Milanese, 1975)

Arendt, Hannah, *The Human Condition* (Chicago: University of Chicago Press, 1998).

Aristotle, Book Q, *Metaphysics*, trans., John Warrington, Everyman's Library (Letchworth: The Aldine Press, 1956)

Aureli, Pier Vittorio, *More and More about Less and Less: Notes Towards a History of Nonfigurative Architecture*, Log 16, ed. Cynthia Davidson (New York: Anycorp, 2009)

Aureli, Pier Vittorio, Unger's Berlin and Green Archipelago, 'Toward the Archipelago,' in *Log 11* ed. Cynthia Davidson (New York: Anycorp, 2008)

Auster, Paul, *New York Trilogy* (London: Faber and Faber, 1987).

Badiou, Alain, with Nicolas Trong, In *Praise of Love*, trans. Peter Bush (London: Serpent's Tail; Profile Books, 2012)

Baird, George, *The Space of Appearance*, (Cambridge MA: MIT Press, 2003)

Bataille, Georges, *The Encyclopaedia Acephalica*, ed. Alastair Brotchie (London: Atlas Press, 1995).

Bataille, Georges, The Notion of Expenditure, in *The Bataille Reader*, ed. Fred Botting and Scott Wilson (London: Blackwell, 1997) pp. 167-187

Bateson, Gregory, *Steps to an Ecology of Mind* (Chicago: University of Chicago Press, 2000)

Baudrillard, Jean, The Rise of the Object: The End of Culture, in *Mass, Identity, Architecture, Architectural Writings of Jean Baudrillard*, ed. Francesco Proto, (London: Wiley, 2006) pp.95-121.

Benjamin, Walter, *Illuminations*, ed. Hannah Arendt, (London: Fontana Press, 1992).

Benjamin, Walter, *Reflections, Essays, Aphorisms, Autobiographical Writings*, trans. Edmund Jephcott, ed. Peter Demetz (New York: Schocken Books, 1986).

Benjamin, Walter, *Understanding Brecht*, trans. Anna Bostock (London: Verso, 1983).

Benjamin, Walter, *Walter Benjamin, Selected Writings*, vol. 2, part 1, 1927-1930, trans. Rodney Livingstone and others, ed. Michael W. Jennings, Howard Eiland and Gary Smith (Cambridge, MA: The Belknap Press of Harvard University Press, 2005).

Bhabha, Homi, *The Location of Culture* (Abingdon: Routledge, 2005)

Blanchot, Maurice, *The Station Hill Blanchot Reader, Fiction and Literary Essays* (New York: Station Hill Press, 1999).

Hegel, G.W.F.,*Philosophy of Right* (1820), trans. S.W. Hyde (New York: Dover Publications, Inc., 2005)

Heidegger, Martin, Building, Dwelling, Thinking, in *Poetry, Language, Thought*,trans. Albert Hofstadter (New York: Perennial, 2001).

Hejduk, John, *Mask of Medussa,* (New York: Rizzoli International, 1985)

Jarry Alfred, *Exploits and Opinions of Dr. Faustroll, Pataphysician, A Neo-Scientific Novel*, trans. Simon Watson Taylor (Boston: Exact Change, 1996).

Kagis-McEwan, Indra, *Socrates' Ancestor, An Essay on Architectural Beginnings* (Cambridge, MA: MIT Press, 1993).

Kant, Immanuel, *What is Enlightenment?* (1784), http://philosophy.eserver.org/kant/what-is-enlightenment.txt

Koolhaus, Rem, Advancement versus Apocalypse, in *Ecological Urbanism*, eds. Mohsen Mostafavi and Gareth Doherty (Lars Müllers Publishers: Baden, Switzerland, 2010) pp.56-71.

Kristeva, Julia, *Revolution in Poetic Language* (New York: Columbia University Press, 1984)

Lampadusa, *The Leopard*

Latour, Bruno, ''Where Are the Missing Masses? The Sociology of a Few Mundane Artefacts.'' http://www.bruno-latour.fr/articles/article/50-MISSING-MASSESrepub.pdf

Latour, Bruno, *The Berlin Key or How to Do Words with Things*', http://www.bruno-latour.fr/poparticles/poparticle/p036.html

Lawrence, D. H., *Sea and Sardinia*

Lefebvre, Henri, *Key Writings*, ed. Stuart Elden, Elizabeth Lebas and Eleonore Kofman (New York, London: Continuum, 2003).

Lévinas, Émmanuel, *Collected Philosophical Papers*, trans. Alphonso Lingis (Dordrecht: Martinus Nijhoff Publishers, 1987).

Lévinas, Émmanuel, *Emmanual Levinas, Basic Philosophical Writings*, ed. Peperzak, Critchley and Bernasconi (Bloomington: Indiana University Press, 1996).

Lévinas, Émmanuel, *Face to Face With Levinas*, ed., Richard Cohen (Albany: State University of New York Press, 1986).

Lévinas, Émmanuel, *Otherwise Than Being or Beyond Essence*, trans. Alphonso Lingis (Dordrecht and Boston: Kluwer Academic Publishers, 1974).

Lévinas, Émmanuel, *Outside The Subject*, trans. Michael B. Smith, ed. Werner Hamacher & David E. Wellbery (Palo Alto: Stanford University Press, 1994).

Lévinas, Émmanuel, *Totality and Infinity*, trans. Alphonso Lingis (Pittsburgh: Duquesne University Press, 1969).

Lévinas, Émmanuel, *Unforeseen History*, trans. Nidra Poller (Illinois: University of Illinois Press, 2004).

Marx, Karl, The Grundrisse (The Foundations of The Critique Into Political Economy, 1856), in *The Marx Engels Reader* (New York: W. W. Norton & Company, 1978)

Marx, Karl, *The Marx Engels Reader*, ed. Robert C. Tucker (New York: W. W. Norton & Company, 1978).

More, Thomas, *Utopia* (1516) (Cambridge: CUP 1989).

Mostafavi, Mohsen, *Ecological Urbanism*, eds. Mohsen Mostafavi and Gareth Doherty (Lars Müllers Publishers: Baden, Switzerland, 2010)

Perec, George, *Life A User's Manual*, trans. David Bellos (London: The Harvill Press, 1987).

Perec, George, *Species of Spaces and Other Pieces*, (London: Penguin Books, 1999).

Perez-Gomez, Alberto, *Architecture and The Crisis of Modern Science* (Cambridge MA: MIT Press, 1983).

Plato, The Sophist.

Popper, Karl,*The Open Society and its Enemies* (London: Routledge, 2011)

Quanrill, Malcolm, *Plain Modern, The Architecture of Brian Mackay-Lyons* (New York: Princeton Architectural Press, 2005).

Rancière, Jacques, *The Emancipated Spectator*, trans. Gregory Elliot (London: Verso, 2009)

Rancière, Jacques, *The Politics of Aesthetics, The Distribution of The Sensible*, trans. Gabriel Rockhill (London: Continuum, 2005)

Ricoeur, Paul, *A Ricoeur Reader, Reflection and Imagination*, ed. Mario J. Valdés (Toronto: University of Toronto Press, 1991).

Ricoeur, Paul, *Memory, History, Forgetting*, trans. Kathleen Blamey and David Pellauer (Chicago: University of Chicago Press, 2006).

Rossi, Aldo, *Selected Writing and Projects*, ed. John O'Reagan (London: Architectural Design, 1983).

Rossi, Aldo, *The Architecture of The City* (Cambridge MA: MIT Press, 1984)

Serres, Michel, *China Loam, in Detachment*, trans. Genevieve James and Raymond Federman (Columbas: Ohio State University Press, 1989)

Serres, Michel, *Genesis*, trans. Genevieve James and James Nelson (Ann Arbor: University of Michigan Press, 1995).

Serres, Michel, *The Natural Contract*, trans Elizabeth MacAtrhur and William Paulson (Ann Arbor: University of Michigan Press, 2008).

Serres, Michel, *The Parasite*, trans Lawrence R. Schehr (Minnesota: University Of Minnesota Press, 2007).

Simmel, Georg, *The Stranger, The Sociology of Georg Simmel*, ed. K.H. Wolff, (Glencoe [Illinois]: Free Press, 1950) pp.402-408.

Swift, Jonathan, *Gulliver's Travels*

Tafuri, Manfredo, *The Sphere and The Labyrinth, Avant Gardes and Architecture from Piranesi to the 1970s*, trans. Pellegrino d'Acierno and Robert Connolly (Cambridge, MA: MIT Press, 1987).

Tafuri, Manfredo, *Theories and History of Architecture*, trans. Giorgio Verrecchia (New York: Harper & Row, 1980).

Vesely, Dalibor, *Architecture In The Age of Divided Representation, The Question of Creativity In The Shadow of Production* (Cambridge Massachusetts: MIT Press, 2004).

Vitruvius, *The Ten Books on Architecture*, trans. Morris Hicky Morgan (New York: Dover Books, 1961).

Waldheim, Charles, *Notes Toward a History of Agrarian Urbanism*, http://brkt.org/index.php/soft/entry/notes_towards_a_history_of_agrarian_urbanism

Wall, Thomas Carl, *Radical Passivity, Levinas, Blanchot and Agamben* (Albany: State University of New York Press, 1999).

Wiszniewski, D. and Thomson, H., *Pyrotechnic Peonies: Portobello's New Marine Gardens*, in 6000 miles, (Glasgow: The Lighthouse, 2005) pp. 24-35 [ISBN 1-90561-05-6]

Wiszniewski, D., *Architecture & Series*, ed. D. Wiszniewski (Ampersand Publishing, Architecture University of Edinburgh: Edinburgh, Spring 2011) ISBN: 9780955970689.

Wiszniewski, D., Beyond Architecture: Architecture and Immateriality, in *Athens by Sound, Greek Pavilion Exhibition Book - 11th Architecture Biennale of Venice*, Authors and Eds: A. Karandinou, C. Achtypi, S. Giamarelos. (Athens: Futura Publications, 2008). ISBN 9789606654801 pp. 48-52.

Wiszniewski, D., *Borderlands in Istanbul: Tectonics and The Politics of Gesture*, Toplumbilim, Vol. 22, May (October) 2007, ed. Yayin Kurulu Baskani, (Istanbul: Hamur, 2007) pp. 185-208. (ISSN-1301-0468)

Wiszniewski, D., City as Museum: Museum as City, Mediating The Everyday and Special Narratives of Life, in *Narrative Space/Museum Making*, eds. Jonathan Hale, Laura Hanks and Suzanne McLeod (London: Routledge, 2012). pp 119-132

Wiszniewski, D., Coyne, R., 'From Questionable Ethics to Sound Judgements', in *34th European Association of Architectural Education Workshop*: "Ethics in Architecture: Architectural Education in the Epoch of Virtuality", (Denmark: Aarhus School of Architecture and European Association for Architectural Education) pp. 103-117 [ISBN 2-930301-02-3]

Wiszniewski, D., *Florence: Curating The City*, ed Dorian Wiszniewski (Architecture, University of Edinburgh: Edinburgh, 2010) [ISBN 978-0-9559706-7-2]

Wiszniewski, D., Levinas And Architecture, (2009), in *LÉVINAS, CHINESE AND WESTERN PERSPECTIVES*, ed. Cheng and Bunnin, Book Supplement Series to the Journal of Chinese Philosophy, Volume 35, (Oxford: Wiley-Blackwell, March 2009) pp. ISBN-10: 1405195452; ISBN-13: 9781405195454.

Wiszniewski, D., R.Coyne and C. Pierce, Turing's Machines, in *Architectural Computing from Turing to 2000*, Proceedings from 17th conference on eCAADe (Liverpool: Liverpool University Press, 1999) pp.25-31.

Wiszniewski, D., *Seriality And The Radically Passive Encounter With Buildings: The Everyday Process Of Reading Architecture - The Geometry And Gesturality Of Lamb's House*, Leith, Scotland, in The Nexus Network Journal, Geometry and Rhetoric, Volume 12, Issue 3 (Basel: Birkhauser Verlag and Springer, 2010) pp. 421-443. [DOI: 10.1007/s00004-010-0048-y] http://www.springerlink.com/content/12q1638731662136/

Wiszniewski, D., Tectonics and the Space of Communicativity, in *Contribution and Confusion: Architecture and the Influence of Other Fields of Enquiry*, (New York: ACSA Press, 2004) pp. 423-431 [ISBN 0-935502-55-6]

Wiszniewski, D., The Space of Communicativity; Levinas And Architecture (Chinese Language), in *A Century With Levinas or Destiny of the Other*, ed. Nicholas Bunnin and Simon Critchley, (Renmin University Press, China, 2008) pp.457-468. [ISBN 978-7-300-09536-3/B.575].

Wiszniewski, Dorian and Richard Coyne, Mask and Identity, The Hermenutics of Self-Construction in the Information Age, in *Building Virtual Communities, Learning and Change in Cyberspace*, eds. K. Ann Renninger and Wesley Shumar (Cambridge: Cambridge University Press, 2002) pp.191-214.

Wiszniewski, Dorian, *Borderlands in Istanbul: Tectonics and The Politics of Gesture*, Toplumbilim, Vol. 22, ed. YayinKuruluBaskani, May (October) 2007

Wood, Sharon, *Essays on Grazia Deledda*, ed. Sharon Wood (Leicester: Troubador Publishing, 2007)

Serres, Michel, *Genesis*, trans. Genevieve James and James Nelson (Ann Arbor: University of Michigan Press, 1995).

Serres, Michel, *The Natural Contract*, trans Elizabeth MacAtrhur and William Paulson (Ann Arbor: University of Michigan Press, 2008).

Serres, Michel, *The Parasite*, trans Lawrence R. Schehr (Minnesota: University Of Minnesota Press, 2007).

Simmel, Georg, *The Stranger, The Sociology of Georg Simmel*, ed. K.H. Wolff, (Glencoe [Illinois]: Free Press, 1950) pp.402-408.

Swift, Jonathan, *Gulliver's Travels*

Tafuri, Manfredo, *The Sphere and The Labyrinth, Avant Gardes and Architecture from Piranesi to the 1970s*, trans. Pellegrino d'Acierno and Robert Connolly (Cambridge, MA: MIT Press, 1987).

Tafuri, Manfredo, *Theories and History of Architecture*, trans. Giorgio Verrecchia (New York: Harper & Row, 1980).

Vesely, Dalibor, *Architecture In The Age of Divided Representation, The Question of Creativity In The Shadow of Production* (Cambridge Massachusetts: MIT Press, 2004).

Vitruvius, *The Ten Books on Architecture*, trans. Morris Hicky Morgan (New York: Dover Books, 1961).

Waldheim, Charles, *Notes Toward a History of Agrarian Urbanism*, http://brkt.org/index.php/soft/entry/notes_towards_a_history_of_agrarian_urbanism

Wall, Thomas Carl, *Radical Passivity, Levinas, Blanchot and Agamben* (Albany: State University of New York Press, 1999).

Wiszniewski, D. and Thomson, H., *Pyrotechnic Peonies: Portobello's New Marine Gardens*, in 6000 miles, (Glasgow: The Lighthouse, 2005) pp. 24-35 [ISBN 1-90561-05-6]

Wiszniewski, D., *Architecture & Series*, ed. D. Wiszniewski (Ampersand Publishing, Architecture University of Edinburgh: Edinburgh, Spring 2011) ISBN: 9780955970689.

Wiszniewski, D., Beyond Architecture: Architecture and Immateriality, in *Athens by Sound, Greek Pavilion Exhibition Book - 11th Architecture Biennale of Venice*, Authors and Eds: A. Karandinou, C. Achtypi, S. Giamarelos. (Athens: Futura Publications, 2008). ISBN 9789606654801 pp. 48-52.

Wiszniewski, D., *Borderlands in Istanbul: Tectonics and The Politics of Gesture*, Toplumbilim, Vol. 22, May (October) 2007, ed. Yayin Kurulu Baskani, (Istanbul: Hamur, 2007) pp. 185-208. (ISSN-1301-0468)

Wiszniewski, D., City as Museum: Museum as City, Mediating The Everyday and Special Narratives of Life, in *Narrative Space/Museum Making*, eds. Jonathan Hale, Laura Hanks and Suzanne McLeod (London: Routledge, 2012). pp 119-132

Wiszniewski, D., Coyne, R., 'From Questionable Ethics to Sound Judgements', in *34th European Association of Architectural Education Workshop*: "Ethics in Architecture: Architectural Education in the Epoch of Virtuality", (Denmark: Aarhus School of Architecture and European Association for Architectural Education) pp. 103-117 [ISBN 2-930301-02-3]

Wiszniewski, D., *Florence: Curating The City*, ed Dorian Wiszniewski (Architecture, University of Edinburgh: Edinburgh, 2010) [ISBN 978-0-9559706-7-2]

Wiszniewski, D., Levinas And Architecture, (2009), in LÉVINAS, *CHINESE AND WESTERN PERSPECTIVES*, ed. Cheng and Bunnin, Book Supplement Series to the Journal of Chinese Philosophy, Volume 35, (Oxford: Wiley-Blackwell, March 2009) pp. ISBN-10: 1405195452; ISBN-13: 9781405195454.

Wiszniewski, D., R.Coyne and C. Pierce, Turing's Machines, in *Architectural Computing from Turing to 2000*, Proceedings from 17ᵗʰ conference on eCAADe (Liverpool: Liverpool University Press, 1999) pp.25-31.

Wiszniewski, D., *Seriality And The Radically Passive Encounter With Buildings: The Everyday Process Of Reading Architecture - The Geometry And Gesturality Of Lamb's House*, Leith, Scotland, in The Nexus Network Journal, Geometry and Rhetoric, Volume 12, Issue 3 (Basel: Birkhauser Verlag and Springer, 2010) pp. 421-443. [DOI: 10.1007/s00004-010-0048-y] http://www.springerlink.com/content/12q1638731662136/

Wiszniewski, D., Tectonics and the Space of Communicativity, in *Contribution and Confusion: Architecture and the Influence of Other Fields of Enquiry*, (New York: ACSA Press, 2004) pp. 423-431 [ISBN 0-935502-55-6]

Wiszniewski, D., The Space of Communicativity; Levinas And Architecture (Chinese Language), in *A Century With Levinas or Destiny of the Other*, ed. Nicholas Bunnin and Simon Critchley, (Renmin University Press, China, 2008) pp.457-468. [ISBN 978-7-300-09536-3/B.575].

Wiszniewski, Dorian and Richard Coyne, Mask and Identity, The Hermenutics of Self-Construction in the Information Age, in *Building Virtual Communities, Learning and Change in Cyberspace*, eds. K. Ann Renninger and Wesley Shumar (Cambridge: Cambridge University Press, 2002) pp.191-214.

Wiszniewski, Dorian, *Borderlands in Istanbul: Tectonics and The Politics of Gesture*, Toplumbilim, Vol. 22, ed. YayinKuruluBaskani, May (October) 2007

Wood, Sharon, *Essays on Grazia Deledda*, ed. Sharon Wood (Leicester: Troubador Publishing, 2007)

Credits

Edinburgh Students.

(Amy) Li Bingxin (LB) MSc AUD
Louisa Butler (LB) MArch
Neil Cunning (NC) MArch
Jørgen Ekerhøvd (JE) MArch
Mathew Gauci (MW) MSc AUD
Xiaorui Ge (XG) MArch
(Kittie) Sinling Hoe (SH) MArch
Ryan Hodge (RH) MArch
Angel Hsiao (AH) MArch
(Jane) Zheng Huang (ZH) MSc AUD
Melinda Jin (MJ) MArch
(Simon) Su Junhua (SJ) MSc AUD
Jamie Kinghorn (JK) MArch
(Jak) Weifeng Kong (WK) MArch
(Ethan) Huining Li (HuL) MSc AUD
(Li) He Li (HL) MSc AUD
(Sherry) Yi Liu (YL) MSc AUD
(Emiline) Mi Lin (ML) MSc AUD
Paul MacDonald (PM) MArch
Li Maili (LM) MSc AUD
Elvira Marina (EM) MArch
Ruth Marsh (RM) MArch
Craig McLeish (CMl) MArch
Caterina Mendolicchio (CM) MSc AUD
Stephen Micallef (SM) MSc AUD

Mohsen Najafian (MN) MArch
Nia Puliyel (NP) MArch
Jennifer Robertson (JR) MArch
Shiyun Shen (SS) MArch
(Katie) Quing Shoa (QS) MSc AUD
Anirudh Sood (AS) MArch
Rachel Stancliffe (RS) MArch
Barbara Swierc (BS) MArch
Scott Wallace (SW) MArch
Siyu Wang (SYW) MArch
(Way) Jinwu Wei (JW) MSc AUD
(Eric) Yucong Wen (YW) MSc AUD
Oliver Wit (OW) MArch
Douglas Wright (DJW) MArch
(How) Hao Wu (HW) MSc AUD
Lynda Zein (LZ) MArch
(Wendy) Sixiao Zhang (SZ) MSc AUD
(Tina) Boya Zhang (BZ) MSc AUD
(John) Zhe Zhang (ZZ) MSc AUD
(Neo) Pengfeng Zhang (PZ) MSc AUD

Students in Alghero, Sardinia.

Salvatore Cambilargiu
Fabio Campus
Alessandra Craboledda
Denis Cuccu
Anna Cuccuru
Giovanna Diana
Mario Doneddu
Ilaria Fadda
Silvia Lai
Sara Mantega
Mariella Masala
Nino Ondradu
Giovanni Ortu
Margherita Perrod
Baldassarre Riu
Daniele Ruiu
Antonio Secondo
Davide Sechi
Giuseppe Zingaro

THE UNIVERSITY of EDINBURGH
Edinburgh College of Art

Facoltà di Architettura
Università degli Studi di Sassari

Edinburgh Studio Tutors.

Kevin Adams
Yael Hameiri (YH) *(Visiting Scholar)*
Paul Pattinson
Dorian Wiszniewski (DW)

Tutors in Alghero, Sardinia.

Kevin Adams
Samanta Bartocci
Elio Bedarida
Mimmo Biddau
Christian Cannaos
Yael Hameiri
Antonnello Marotta
Francesca Rango
Verdina Satta
Silvia Serreli
Michele Valentino

International Visitors/ Critics/Scholars.

Dorian Wiszniewski
Kevin Adams
Samanta Bartocci
Nora Bateson
Tom Brooksbank
Ella Chmielewska
Chris Freemantle
Chris French
Yael Hameiri
Tahl Kaminer
Piotr Lesniak
Laura Lutzoni
Valeria Monno
Ross McLean
Maria Mitsoula
Paul Pattinson
Francesca Rango (FR)
Peg Rawes
Liam Ross
Verdina Satta
Silvia Serreli
Michele Valentino (MV)
Dorian Wiszniewski
Lisa Young

Editorial and Graphic Design.

Jamie Kinghorn
Paul MacDonald
Allyson Pattie
Dorian Wiszniewski

Printed by
Barr Printers
Dock Place,
Edinburgh,
EH6 6LU

Acknowledgements.

Credit also goes to all academic, administrative and technical staff who have helped deliver courses as part of the M Arch and M Sc AUD 2011-2012 programmes within the University of Edinburgh.

Order Information:
e: dorian.wiszniewski@ed.ac.uk

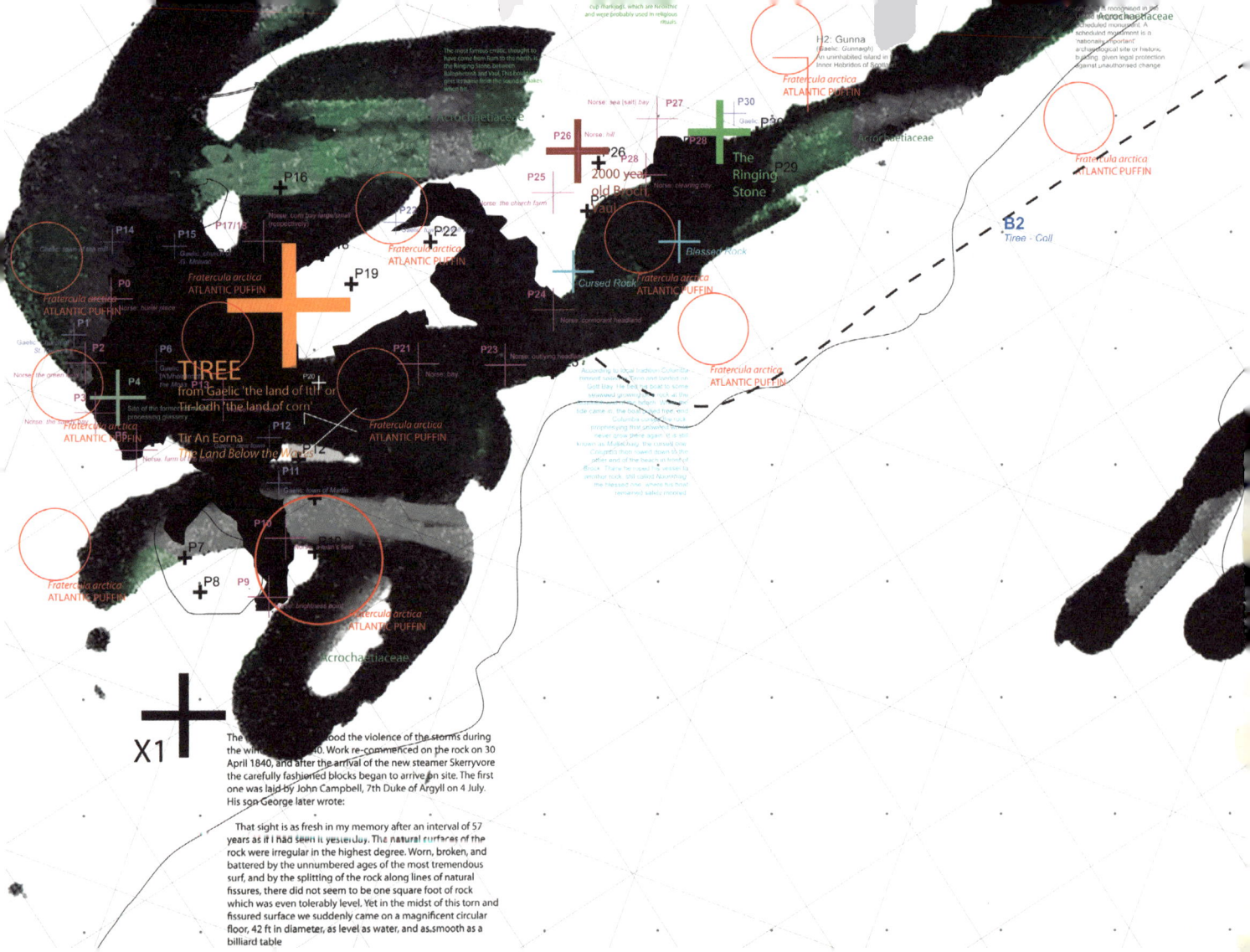

The most famous erratic, thought to
have come from Rum to the north, is
the Ringing Stone, between
Balephetrish and Vaul. This boulder
rings strangely from the sounds it makes
when hit.

cup markings, which are notable
and were probably used in religious
rituals.

It is recognised in the
list of the scheduled
monuments. A
scheduled monument is a
'nationally important'
archaeological site or feature,
typically, given legal protection
against unauthorised change

H2: Gunna
(Gaelic: Gunnagh)
An uninhabited island in
Inner Hebrides of Scotland

Fratercula arctica
ATLANTIC PUFFIN

Acrochaetiaceae

Norse: sea (salt) bay   P27   P30
Gaelic: Pè...
Norse: hill
P26   P28
P26   The
P25   2000 year   Ringing   P29
old Brooch   Stone
... ul

Fratercula arctica
ATLANTIC PUFFIN

B2
Tiree - Coll

Fratercula arctica
ATLANTIC PUFFIN

P16

P14   P15   P17/18

Norse: corn bay large/small
(respectively)   P22
Norse: the church farm

Fratercula arctica
ATLANTIC PUFFIN

Blessed Rock

Gaelic: church of
G. Moluag

Fratercula arctica
ATLANTIC PUFFIN

P19

Cursed Rock

Fratercula arctica
ATLANTIC PUFFIN

Fratercula arctica
ATLANTIC PUFFIN   P0

Norse: burial maze

Norse: the church farm

Norse: cormorant headland

P1

Gaelic: ...
St. Patrick's

P2   P6

P4   Gaelic: town
[Aird]
the Mora   P13

Norse: outlying headland

Fratercula arctica
ATLANTIC PUFFIN

TIREE
from Gaelic 'the land of Ith' or
Tir-Iodh 'the land of corn'

Norse: the green

Fratercula arctica
ATLANTIC PUFFIN

P3   Site of the former
processing glassery

P21   P23   Norse: bay

P20

Tir An Eorna
The Land Below the Waves

P12

Fratercula arctica
ATLANTIC PUFFIN

Norse: farm of the...   P12

According to local tradition, Columba
himself was a pilgrim and landed on
Soft Bay. He had the boat to some
seaweed-grown rock at the
southern end of the harbour. After the
tide came in, the boat floated free, and
Columba utterned a rock
prophesying that seaweed would
never grow there again. It is still
known as Mullachaig, the cursed one.
Clogmate fixed down to the
other end of the harbour to find a
rock. There he raised his vessel to
another rock, still called Naomhthag
the blessed one, where his boat
remained safely moored.

P11
Gaelic: town of Martin

P10

P7

Rubha ...
Norse: dream's field

P8   P9

Fratercula arctica
ATLANTIC PUFFIN

Fratercula arctica
ATLANTIC PUFFIN

Norse: brightness point

Acrochaetiaceae

X1

The ... stood the violence of the storms during
the winter ... 40. Work re-commenced on the rock on 30
April 1840, and after the arrival of the new steamer Skerryvore
the carefully fashioned blocks began to arrive on site. The first
one was laid by John Campbell, 7th Duke of Argyll on 4 July.
His son George later wrote:

That sight is as fresh in my memory after an interval of 57
years as if I had seen it yesterday. The natural surfaces of the
rock were irregular in the highest degree. Worn, broken, and
battered by the unnumbered ages of the most tremendous
surf, and by the splitting of the rock along lines of natural
fissures, there did not seem to be one square foot of rock
which was even tolerably level. Yet in the midst of this torn and
fissured surface we suddenly came on a magnificent circular
floor, 42 ft in diameter, as level as water, and as smooth as a
billiard table